LEGAL TRAIL SERIES®

PROPERTY

Mclaren Legal Publishers
New York

ALSO AVAILABLE IN THIS SERIES:

Civil Procedure
Constitutional Law
Contracts
Criminal Law
Criminal Procedure
Evidence
Property
Torts

LEGAL TRAIL SERIES®

PROPERTY

First Edition

Peter R. Errico, Esq.

New York Law School

ISBN 0-9776210-5-7

Published by
Mclaren Legal Publishers LLC
136 West 21 Street, 8th Floor
New York, NY 10011

www.mclarenpublishing.com
Email: contact@mclarenpublishing.com

Printed in the United States of America

HOW TO USE THIS BOOK

This law school study aid is a non-keyed book. While it includes many of the key critical cases in the subject addressed, it is meant to provide an overall rigorous review of the topic indicated and convey key concepts and points of law for general study. For a keyed book linked to a specific casebook, please use our Legal Path Series® of keyed books.

"Why are there so many detailed cases?"

We've included detailed illustrative cases which are explanative of the topics discussed. We have done so in as concisely but as detailed a manner as we can to provide the legal context and factual background for the point of law illustrated. Often, we have found that a law student's final exam will track a ***similar*** fact pattern to a decisive case in the area discussed. Therefore, if you see the Facts, Rule & Analysis in great detail, you will be better able to apply the same rule of law to a similar but different fact pattern testing the same rule of law.

"All of what you need, none of what you don't"

Our law school study guides give you exactly what you need to understand the key principles of the subject, including the sometimes elusive Black Letter law. We are not a replacement for an in depth legal analysis of the subject matter covered; however, we do present what is absolutely critical in a very concise format.

"Centered, Capitalized and Underlined Headers"

Before a group of cases (and sometimes the individual cases themselves), we have often included a capitalized, centered and underlined header which is illustrative of the key point(s) of law discussed in the preceding chapter/section. For example, after the chapter on defamation, in the Legal Trail Torts book, we have included the following header:

NATURE OF THE DEFAMATORY COMMUNICATION

This header precedes the case, *Belli v. Orlando Daily Newspapers Inc.* which illustrates some aspect of the "nature of the defamatory communication." Where no header is present, general points of law are discussed which again refer back to the preceding section/chapter.

Abbreviations used in this book

I This symbol "I" stands for "Issue"

R This symbol "R" stands for "Rule"

A This symbol "A" stands for "Analysis"

C This symbol "C" stands for "Conclusion"

* Use of the word "his" in this book is gender neutral and encompasses both "his" and "her."

TABLE OF CONTENTS

REAL PROPERTY

I. PRESENT POSSESSORY ESTATES

An estate is an interest in land that may or may not become possessory. Land can be owned by more than one person, each with separate and distinct interests, but at any given time only one possessory estate may exist.

A. Fee Simple Absolute

An interest in land that is in fee simple absolute is indefeasible. Indefeasible means that there is an absolute ownership of the entire interest- present and future, without divestment. In other words, a fee simple absolute is an interest in land that has no restrictions and has a potentially indefinite duration. It can be freely devisable (can pass by will), decendible (can pass by intestacy) and alienable (transferable during the holder's lifetime).

A fee simple absolute interest is created with words such as "to A and his heirs." However, most states today do not require such precise language to create the interest. Today, a fee simple absolute interest is presumed unless otherwise provided.

Under the Rule in Shelly's Case, if an instrument creates a life estate in A and purports to create a remainder in A's heirs, then the remainder becomes a remainder in fee simple.

B. Life Estate

A life estate is an estate that lasts for as long as the possessor lives. As soon as the possessor dies, the estate either reverts back to the grantor or to a third party. A life interest is created using the language, "to A for his life," or "for A's life, then to B." The length of the estate could also be measured by the life of another person. For example, language such as "to A for the life of B," creates a life estate *per autre vie* (for the life of another).

C. **Fee Tail**
A fee tail is an interest in land that attempts to keep property in a family from generation to generation. However, it is no longer a valid interest today.

A fee tail is created with language such as "to A and the heirs of his body." Today, an attempt to create a fee tail is presumed to create a life estate.

D. **Fee Simple Determinable**
A fee simple determinable is an estate that automatically ends. The grantor has a possibility of reverter upon the stated event. A fee simple determinable estate is devisable, decendible, and alienable.

A fee simple determinable is created with such language as "so long as," "while," and "until." For example, language such as "to A so long as it is used for charity," creates a fee simple determinable estate.

E. **Fee Simple Subject to a Condition Subsequent**
A fee simple subject to a condition subsequent is an interest in land where the grantor has the right to reenter when a certain condition occurs.

A fee simple subject to a condition subsequent is created with language such as "upon condition that," "provided that," and "but if X happens." For example, language such as "to B, but if X occurs back to A," creates a fee simple subject to a condition subsequent.

F. **Fee Simple Subject to an Executory Interest**
A fee simple subject to an executory interest is the same as a fee simple subject to a condition subsequent except that the estate passes to a stated third party instead of to the grantor.

A fee simple subject to an executory interest is created the same way as a fee simple subject to a condition subsequent. For example, language such as "to A, but if X occurs, to C," creates a fee simple subject to an executory interest.

PROPERTY

ESTATE	DEFINITION	CREATION	TRANSFERABILITY	FUTURE INTEREST
Fee Simple Absolute	An estate with potentially indefinite duration.	To A and his heirs.	Devisable, decendible, and alienable.	None.
Life Estate	An estate in a person until he dies.	To A for life or to A for the life of B (per autre vie).		Reversion back to the grantor or his heirs.
Fee Simple Determinable	Estate that automatically reverts back to the grantor upon a stated event.	To A and his heirs, so long as the property is used for X.	Devisable, decendible, and alienable.	Possibility of reverter to grantor.
Fee Simple Subject to a Condition Subsequent	Grantor could retake estate upon a stated event.	To A, but if X occurs, then to grantor.	Back to grantor if condition occurs.	Right of reentry.
Fee Simple Subject to an Executory Interest	If stated condition occurs, interest goes to 3rd party.	To A, but if X occurs, to B.	To 3rd party if event occurs.	Shifting or springing executory interest discussed later.
Fee Tail	Estate goes to the decendent of a particular person.	To A and the heirs of his body.	Creation of a fee tail created a fee simple absolute instead.	Reversion to the grantor or Remainder if it goes to a 3rd party.

THE LIFE ESTATE

White v. Brown

(1977) 559 S.W.2d 938

FACTS

Mrs. Jesse Lide died on February 15, 1973, leaving a holographic will (an unwitnessed handwritten will). The will read, in part: "I wish Evelyn White (plaintiff) to have my home to live in and not to be sold… my house is not to be sold." Plaintiff White, her husband, who was the testatrix's brother, and her daughter, Sandra White Perry, lived with Mrs. Lide as a family for some 25 years. After Sandra married in 1969, and Miss White's husband died in 1971, Evelyn White continued to live with Mrs. Lide until Mrs. Lide's death in 1973 at the age of 88. Mrs. White, joined by her daughter as executrix, filed this action to obtain construction of the will, alleging that she is vested with a fee simple title to the home. The Defendants Brown, Mrs. Lide's heirs, claimed that the will conveyed only a life estate to Mrs. White, leaving the remainder to go to them under our laws of intestate succession. The trial court held that the will, on its face, unambiguously conveyed a life estate. No extrinsic evidence was considered by the court.

I Does the will's conveyance of the home to Mrs. White "to live in" give her a life interest or a fee in the home? Or, alternatively, does Mrs. Lide's will, taken as a whole, clearly evidence her intent to convey only a life estate in her home to Mrs. White?

R A will conveys a testator's entire interest unless a contrary intention appears by the will's terms and context.

A Historically, the presumption that a testator conveyed only a life estate existed at common law. However, our Legislature has enacted two statutes which create a statutory presumption against partial intestacy and reverses the common law presumption that a life estate was intended unless the intent to pass a fee simple was clearly expressed in the will. Thus, a will shall convey all the real estate belonging to the testator unless a contrary intention appears by the terms of the will, its words and its context. Several cases demonstrate the effect of these statutory presumptions against intestacy. In *Green v. Young*, the testatrix's disposition of all her property to her husband "to be used by him for his support and comfort during his life" was held to pass a fee simple to the husband. In *Williams v. Williams* the testator's devise of real property to his children "for and during their natural lives" without provision for a gift was held to convey a fee simple. Thus, in the instant case, if the will only contained language that the home was for the plaintiff to live it, a fee simple would pass. However, the language "not to be sold" cause difficulties. Thus, we must look to the context of the will to determine if Lide intended to convey only life estate and where there is ambiguity, we construe a will to dispose of the testator's entire estate, which would be a fee simple in this case. Consequently, it appears that Lide attempted to pass a fee simple to White and further attempted to restrain White from alienating the property. This is evidenced by her words "my house is not to be sold." In our opinion, the testatrix's apparent testimony restraint on alienation of the home devised to Miss White's does not evidence such a clear intent to pass only a life estate as is sufficient to overcome the law's strong presumption that a fee simple interest was conveyed. Accordingly, we conclude that Mrs. Lide's will passed a fee simple absolute in the home to Mrs. White. Mrs. Lide's attempted restraint on alienation must be declared void as inconsistent with public policy. Thus, the decrease of the Court of Appeals and the trial court are reversed and the cause is remanded to the Chancellor record for such further proceedings as may be necessary, consistent with this opinion. Costs are taxed against appellees.

C Yes. A will conveys a testator's entire interest unless a contrary intention appears by the will's terms and context.

Baker v. Weedon

(1972) 262 So. 2d 641; 57 A.L.R.3d 1183

FACTS

John Weedon was married three times: His first marriage to Luka Edwards resulted in two children, Florence and Delette. Florence had three children, Defendants-Appellants Henry, Sarah and Louise. His second marriage was to Ella Howell, resulting in one child, Rachel. Both Rachel and Ella are now deceased. John's third marriage was to Defendant-Appellee Anna Plaxico, who was 17 years old. Anna and John had no children together. John died in 1932. His will left Anna a life estate and his grandchildren a contingent remainder: "I give to my beloved wife… Anna Plaxico… all of my property… during her natural life… and in the event she dies without issue then… I give all property to my grandchildren sharing equally with each other." Anna ceased to farm land in 1955 due to her age and it has been rented ever since. Anna's income from all sources was inadequate to support her. In 1964, the Mississippi State Highway Department sought a right-of-way through the property. The value of the property for commercial purposes was $168,500 at trial. After four years, however, the property's estimated value was placed at $336,000. While Anna now lives in a new home, she is still in economic distress and prays that the property, less the house site, be sold so that she can invest the proceeds to provide her with an adequate income. The plaintiffs wish to stop the proposed immediate sale and allow the property to increase in value before it is sold. The trial court ordered the land sold at a judicial sale because the land was deteriorating and being wasted. The plaintiffs appealed.

I

May a trial court order a judicial sale only if it is "necessary for the best interest of all parties," that is, for both the life tenant and contingent remaindermen?

R

A court should order a judicial sale only if it is in the best interests of both the life tenant and the remaindermen (e.g., holder of the future interest).

A If the circumstances so dictate and the facts so merit, trial courts have jurisdiction to order the sale of land for the prevention of waste. However, we are of the opinion that deterioration and waste of the property is not the exclusive and ultimate test to be used in determining whether a sale of land affected by a future interest is proper, but also that consideration should be given to the question of whether a sale is necessary for the best interests of all the parties: the life tenant and the contingent remainderman. This "necessary for the best interest of all parties," rule is gleaned from *Rogers*, Removal of Future Interest Encumbrances. The law of future interests, §1941, appears to have the necessary flexibility to meet the requirements of usual and unique situations which demand justice and equitable solutions. In this case, a sale would benefit the defendant but create financial loss to the plaintiffs. Thus, a judicial sale is not in the best interest of all parties.

C A court should order a judicial sale only if it is in the best interests of both the life tenant and the remaindermen. Order reversed.

DEFEASIBLE ESTATES

Mahrenholz v. County Board of School Trustees

(1981) 93 Ill. App. 3d 366; 417 N.E.2d 138

FACTS

On March 18, 1941 W.E. and Jennie Hutton executed a warranty deed by which they conveyed (1 ½ acres out of 40 acres they owned) real property to the Trustees of School District No. 1, the predecessors of the defendants in this action. The deed provided that "this land to be used for school purposes only; otherwise to revert to Grantors herein." In July 1941, the Huttons conveyed their reversionary interest (the remaining 38 ½ acres) in this property to Earl and Madeline Jacqmain. In 1959, the Jacqmains conveyed his reversionary interest to put Plaintiff Mahrenholz. The Huttons only legal heir was there son, Harry Hutton.

In 1977, Harry conveyed any Possibility of Reverter or Right of Entry that he may have had in the land to Mahrenholz. Later that same year, Hutton disclaimed any interest he had in the land to the School Board (defendant). This property was used by a school for classes until 1973. Thereafter, the school used the property for storage. Plaintiff argues that the deed conveying the land to the School Board created a Fee Simple Determinable followed by a Possibility of Reverter. The School Board argues that the deed created a fee simple followed by Right of Entry.

I Does language "to be used for school purposes only" create a Fee Simple Determinable or a Fee Simple on Condition Subsequent?

R The language "to be used for school purposes only" creates a Fee Simple Determinable.

A The terms used in the 1941 deed, although imprecise, were designed to allow the property to be used for a single purpose, namely, for "school purposes." The Huttons intended to have the land back if it were ever used otherwise. When a grant of exclusive use followed by an express provision for reverter ceases, courts and commentators have agreed that a fee simple determinable, rather than a fee simple subject to a condition subsequent, is created. The words "so long as the land is used for school purposes" or "while it was used for school purposes" or "until the land ceased to be used for school purposes" create a Fee Simple Determinable. The words "on condition that the land be used for school purposes" or "provided that the land be used for school purposes" create a Fee Simple Subject to Condition Subsequent. In this case, by the express language in the deed, it appears that the Huttons conveyed a Fee Simple Determinable. Since neither a Right of Entry nor a Possibility of Reverter can be transferred by will or inter vivos conveyance, plaintiff could not have acquired the land from Jacqmain. Therefore, we must decide what interest, if any, plaintiff acquired from Harry Hutton. To establish whether a Fee Simple on Condition Subsequent or a Fee Simple Determinable was created, we look at the specific words in the deed. The phrase "for school purposes only" suggests that the Huttons wanted to give the land for only as long as it was needed and no longer. The second part of the expression, "otherwise to revert to the grantor's" seems to indicate an automatic return of the property to the Huttons. Thus, the grant points toward a Fee Simple Determinable. We hold, therefore, that the 1941 deed from W. E. and Janine Hutton to the trustees of School Board District No. 1 created a fee simple determinable in the Trustees followed by a possibility of reverter in the Huttons and their heirs. Accordingly, the trial court erred in dismissing plaintiff's complaint, which followed its holding that the plaintiffs could not have acquired any interest in the Hutton school property from Harry Hutton. Reversed and remanded.

C Yes. The language "to be used for school purposes only" creates a Fee Simple Determinable.

Mountain Brow Lodge No. 82, Independent Order of Odd Fellows v. Toscano

(1968) 257 Cal. App. 2d 22; 64 Cal. Rptr. 816

FACTS

This action was instituted by plaintiff-appellant, a nonprofit corporation, to quiet title to a parcel of real property which it acquired on April 6, 1950 by gift deed from James V. Toscano and Maria Toscano, both deceased. James Toscano was a devoted member of the Mountain Brow Lodge (plaintiff-appellant). Respondents-Defendants are the trustees and administrators of the estates of the deceased grantors (Toscano's heirs). Appellant sought to quiet title as to their interest in the land arising from certain conditions contained in the gift deed. The controversy between the parties centers on the language contained in the habendum clause (that portion of the deed which contains restrictions on the conveyance of the property deeded) of the deed of conveyance. The deed stated that the land was conveyed in consideration of "love and affection" and provided that the lot shall revert back to Toscano if the plaintiff ever failed to use the lot or attempted to sell or transfer it. Respondents maintain that the language creates a fee simple subject to a condition subsequent and is valid and enforceable. Plaintiff-appellant argues that the restrictive language amounts to an absolute restraint on its power of alienation and is thus void. This action follows.

I May the use of land conveyed to another be restricted?

R The use of land conveyed to another may be restricted.

A A restraint on the alienation of land is void as against public policy. Thus, a condition which prohibits appellant from selling or transferring the land under penalty of forfeiture is an absolute restraint against alienation and is thus void. However, a condition relaxing the use of land is clearly severable. In other words, under the plain language of the deed to grantors, their successors or assigns may exercise the power of termination "if the land is not used by the second party" or "in the event of sale or transfer by the second party." Thus, the invalid restraint against alienation does not necessarily affect or nullify the condition on land-use. The outstanding question to be addressed, then, is whether the condition at issue created a defeasible fee. Toscano was a committed Lodge member and he conveyed the land in "loving consideration" containing words which read "the land is restricted for the use of the second party." This clause did not intend to restrict any alienation of the property only regulate how it was to be used; thus creating a fee simple subject to condition subsequent. While restraints on how land may be used can possibly be restraint on who may use the land, such restraints are still allowed in our state.

C Yes. The use of land conveyed to another may be restricted. Judgment declaring restriction on the sale of land reversed.

Ink v. Canton

(1965) 4 Ohio St. 2d 51; 212 N.E.2d 574

FACTS

This case involves the conveyance of a 33 ½ acre track of land known as Ink Park to the City of Canton. Plaintiffs, the descendents of Harry Ink, conveyed this land to the City of Canton (defendants) in 1936. The land was to be used only as a park; no other uses we permitted. The City of Canton adhered to the restrictions in the conveyance and used the land as a park until 1961, when it was condemned by the State of Ohio using its power of eminent domain. The state compensated those with an interest in the land a sum of $130,822. However, plaintiff claimed the right to both the premises and the entire award, arguing that he was justified in doing so since the land was no longer being used as a park. The City of Canton, however, argued that it should get the entire award since it did not voluntarily stop using of the land for park purposes.

I (1) How should the proceeds from an eminent domain proceeding be allocated and (2) what are the rights of the parties with respect to that portion of the property still usable for park purposes?

R The proceeds from an eminent domain proceeding should be allocated between the holder of the fee simple on condition subsequent and the holder of the reverter.

A Where property is conveyed in fee with a stipulation that it is to be used only for a specified use and shall revert to the grantor if such use ceases, it would appear reasonable to conclude that the property would revert when its appropriation by eminent domain proceedings prevents that use. Such a conclusion is reasonable where, as in the instant case, the grantee paid nothing for what had been conveyed to him. Thus, until a court of equity gives authority to do otherwise, the City must hold any interest in the Ink Park property not taken from it subject to the fiduciary obligations imposed upon it by the deed(s) conveying that property to it. Likewise, whatever money the City received in the eminent domain proceedings for the land taken and on account of damages to the Ink Park land not taken can only be held by the City so long as it proposes to use, can reasonably use and does use that money for Ink Park purposes; and any of that money which the city either does not propose to use, cannot reasonably use or does not use for Ink Park purposes should revert to the plaintiffs. It follows that so long as the city proposes to, can reasonably and does use for Ink Park purposes the part of a park property not taken in eminent domain proceedings and the money it receives for park land taken and on account of damages to such land not taken, neither such land no money will revert to plaintiffs although plaintiffs will retain their rights of reverter over with respect to that land and that money. Thus, defendant gets the value of the land with a use restriction and plaintiff gets the value of the land with no restriction less the value of the land with a use restriction. If defendant fails to use its proceeds for park purposes, the money shall revert to the plaintiff.

C The proceeds from an eminent domain proceeding are to be allocated between the holder of the fee simple on condition subsequent and the holder of the reverter.

II. FUTURE INTERESTS

A. Future Interests in Grantor

A future interest in a grantor is a reversionary interest. There are three types of reversionary interests:

1. Reversion

A reversion is an automatic transfer of an interest in property back to the grantor. This arises when the estate in a grantee terminates in a manner other than by a condition.

Under the **Doctrine of Worthier Title**, if a grantor attempted to convey property with a future interest in the grantor's heirs, the future interest is void and the heirs get nothing while the grantor retains a reversion.

2. Possibility of Reverter

A possibility of reverter always deals with a fee simple determinable estate. A possibility of reverter exists if there is a condition on the use of the property. A possibility of reverter differs from a reversion in that a reversion is certain to occur whereas a possibility of reverter may never happen.

3. Right of Reentry

A right of reentry arises when a condition is broken and is seen in conjunction with a fee simple subject to a condition subsequent.

B. Future Interests in Third Parties

1. Remainder Interests

A remainder occurs when a future interest in a third party expires.

a. **Vested Remainder**
A vested remainder is a remainder created in ascertained (known) persons and not subject to a condition subsequent. There are three types of vested remainders:

- **Indefeasible Vested Remainder**
  An indefeasible vested remainder is a future interest certain to become possessory.

- **Vested Remainder Subject to Total Divestment**
  A vested remainder subject to total divestment is a future interest which must vest if a prior possessory interest terminates in time.

- **Vested Remainder Subject to Open**
  A vested remainder subject to open is a future interest which is certain to vest in someone but there is a chance that persons that are not ascertainable may also take and share in the estate.

b. **Contingent Remainder**
A contingent remainder is an estate created in unascertained persons and or subject to a condition precedent.

c. **Executory Interest**
An executory interest is a future interest created in a third party that is not a remainder. There are two types of executory interests:

- **Shifting Executory Interest**
  A shifting executory interest cuts short another's interest who is not the grantor. For example, "To A and his heirs, but if B

returns within a year, to B and his heirs," is a shifting executory interest.

- **Springing Executory Interest**
  A springing executory interest divests the transferor in the future. For example, "To A when he marries B," is a springing executory interest.

Future Interest	**Vested Remainder**	**Contingent Remainder**	**Executory Interest**
Definition	Future interest created in ascertained persons not subject to a condition precedent.	Future interest created in unascertained persons and or subject to a condition precedent.	Future interest created in 3rd parties which is not a remainder.
Variation of the Future Interest	• Indefeasible Vested Remainder • Vested Remainder Subject to Total Divestment		• Shifting Executory Interest • Springing Executory Interest

C. **The Rule against Perpetuities**
The rule against perpetuities states that a future interest is void if there is any possibility that the interest will not vest within 21 years of some life in being at the creation of the interest.

The elements of the rule against perpetuities are:

1. **Vesting**
A vested remainder subject to open vests when the class closes. A contingent remainder vests when the grantee is ascertainable and there are no condition precedents. An executory interest vests when the

parties receive possession. It is not necessary that the interest actually vest but that the vesting does not occur to far in the future. Some states implement the **Wait and See Doctrine**, which states that contingent remainders are not automatically void, but are allowed if they vest within the rule.

1. Twenty-one Year Rule
Conveyance of an interest may not occur more than 21 years after a life in being.

2. Life in Being
A life in being does not have to be the grantor's life, but can be anyone connected to the interest.

3. At the Creation of the Interest
This means that the rule against perpetuities is triggered when the creating instrument takes effect.

THE TRUST

Swanson v. Swanson
(1999) 270 Ga. 733, 514 S.E.2d 822

FACTS

George Swanson died in 1970 and was survived by his wife, Gertrude and nine children. George left a will that created two trusts in which Gertrude had a life estate, the remainder to go to George's nine children. George was predeceased by one of his sons, Bennie, who left everything to his (Bennie's) wife, Plaintiff Laura C. "Peggy" Swanson. After George's death, Peggy attempted to lay claim to her deceased husband's remainder interests in the two trusts. George's wife Gertrude and the other children (collectively the defendants) objected and this action was filed to determine the respective rights of the parties in the trusts.

I Does Laura C. "Peggy" Swanson inherit from her dead husband the remainder interests he had in the two trusts created by his father; or, in the alternative, does the law prefer vested remainders to contingent remainders?

R The law favors construing conditions to be subsequent and remainders to be vested in a court determination as to whether a remainder is contingent or vested.

A To distinguish between vested and contingent remainders, a court must determine whether, at the time an instrument of transfer takes effect, there exists a person who would take all of the transferred property if the life estate ended instantly. If there is such person, the remainder is vested subject to either partial or complete defeasance. If no such person is identifiable, then the remainder subject to a condition precedent and is a contingent remainder. In making a determination between contingent invested remainders, Georgia law has followed two common law principles: (1) the law favors construing conditions to be subsequent and (2) the law favors the vesting of remainders in all cases where there's any doubt as to the nature of the remainder. Trust No. 1 allows Gertrude to dispose of the corpus of the trust either during her life or in her will, but if she fails to do so the corpus passes to George's nine children in equal shares. However, if any of the children should not be alive at the time of her (Gertrude's) death, the share of that deceased child (2nd generation) should go to his or her surviving children (3rd generation), *per stirpes* (a method of dividing an estate among a class of people based on representation at a closer degree of relationship to the deceased person than the degree of the class itself.). After George's death, there were immediately nine identifiable persons (George's nine children) who could take the property if Gertrude's life estate ended. Therefore, each child, Bennie included, had a vested remainder interest. Trust No. 2 also provides for equal distribution among George's nine children. As with the first trust, Bennie's remainder was vested and therefore passed to his wife (Plaintiff Peggy Swanson) upon his death. We hold that Bennie Swanson's 1/9 interest in the trust passes to his wife, his sole heir and beneficiary under his will, because won his remainder was vested; to no condition subsequent occurred prior to the termination of the life estate; three there is no language in the will that plainly he manifests a contrary intent; and for this construction is supported by case law and the applicable common-law principles. Because Bennie Swanson's interest vested before his death and condition subsequent contained in the trust provisions did not occur before the life beneficiary of the trust died, Bennie's vested remainder was not defeased and instead passed according to the terms of his will. Therefore, we reverse.

C The law favors construing conditions to be subsequent and remainders to be vested in a court determination as to whether a remainder is contingent or vested. Reversed.

THE RULE AGAINST PERPETUITIES: THE COMMON LAW RULE

Jee v. Audley

(1787) 1 Cox 324; 29 Eng. Rep. 1186

FACTS

Edward Audley willed an interest in £1000 to his wife for life and upon her death the principle was to go to his niece, Mary hall, in fee tail. However, if Mary Hall died without issue, then the principal was to go to the daughters then living of John and Elizabeth Jee, Edward's relatives. Edward Audley's wife predeceased him and when Edward died, John and Elizabeth Jee were in their 70's and Mary Hall was 40 years old and without children. The Jee daughters (plaintiffs) sued to acquire the principal in the event Mary Hall died without issue. In support of their position, the Jee daughters argued that: (1) since John and Elizabeth Jee are so old, they are unlikely to have more daughters; (2) the class of Jee daughters is fixed and determined; and (3) the interest is not remote and does not violate the rule against perpetuities. Conversely, the Audley Estate (defendant) argues that any interest held by the Jee daughters is void because it violates the letter of the rule against perpetuities.

I Does a living heir who was required to have children during her lifetime in order to receive an interest in £1000 at the time of the testator's death, but who has not, default on the terms of the testator's last will and testament, thereby giving the living nieces full present interest in the money; that is, does the rule against perpetuities consider a "what might happen" scenario at the time the interest is created or "wait and see" if the interest actually vests during the perpetuities period?

R The limitations of personal estate are void, unless they necessarily vest, if at all, within a life or lives in being and 21 years or 9 or 10 months thereafter; the rule against perpetuities considers what might happen at the time an interest is created and does not wait and see if the interest vests during the perpetuities period.

A We hold that as a matter of law that John and Elizabeth Jee are not too old to have children. If we were to hold otherwise, such a decision might set a dangerous precedent. Perhaps a court of the future might hold as a matter of law that a 19 year old couple could not have children. Even so, we must look to see whether the interest was valid when created, not whether it is valid now. Here, the interest in the Jee daughters was void when created because John and Elizabeth might have had children 10 years after Edward died, and then Mary might die without issue 50 years thereafter. Thus, the interest might vest far in the future.

C The rule against perpetuities considers what might happen at the time an interest is created. Judgment for the Audrey Estate.

The Symphony Space, Inc. v. Pergola Properties, Inc.

(1996) 88 N.Y.2d 466, 669 N.E.2d 799, 646 N.Y.S.2d 641

FACTS

In 1978 Plaintiff The Symphony Space Inc. and Broadwest Realty Corp. engaged in a transaction whereby Broadwest sold a building to

Symphony for the below market price of $10,010 and leased back the income producing commercial property, excluding the theater, for $1 per year. Broadwest maintained liability for the existing $243,000 mortgage on the property as well as certain maintenance obligations. As a condition of the sale, Symphony, for consideration of $10, granted Broadwest an option to repurchase the entire building any time after July 1, 1979 and so long as the closing occured during calendar years 1987, 1993, 1998, or 2003. The purpose of this arrangement was to enable Symphony, as a not-for-profit corporation, to seek a property tax exemption for the entire building, predicated on its use of the theater. The sale and lease back would thereby reduce Broadwest's real estate taxes by $30,000 per year but permitting Broadwest to retain the rental income from the leased commercial space in the building of $140,000 annually. Three years after the initiation of the sale/leaseback, Broadwest sold and assigned its interest in the lease, option agreement and mortgage to a 3rd party for $4.8 million. That party then transferred its newly acquired interest to Defendant Pergola Properties Inc. and four other entities as tenants in common. Because the value of the property had increased significantly since the original deal had been signed, the defendant decided to exercise the buy back option. To secure its ownership of the building, the plaintiff filed a declaratory judgment arguing that the option agreement between itself and Broadwest was void under New York's rule against perpetuities. The trial court and intermediate appellate courts sided with Plaintiff The Symphony Space Inc. and Defendant Pergola Properties Inc. appealed to the New York Court of Appeals.

I Under New York statutory law, are options to purchase commercial property exempt from the prohibition against remote vesting in the Rule against Perpetuities?

R There exists no exception to New York's Rule against Perpetuities for commercial option agreements. New York's version of the Rule against Perpetuities measures exclusively by the passage of time, while the common law rule evaluates the reasonableness of the restraint based on its duration, purpose and designated method for fixing the purchase price.

A New York's version of the Rule against Perpetuities (1) limits control of title to real property by dead landowners who seek to reach into future generations; and (2) ensures the productive use and development of property by its current beneficial owners by simplifying ownership, facilitating exchange and freeing property from impediments to alienability. New York's current statutory Rule against Perpetuities is found in EPTL. 9-1.1. It contains two subsections relevant to the instant action. Subsection (a) voids any estate in which the conveying instrument suspends the absolute power of alienation for longer than some lives in being at the creation of the estate plus 21 years while subsection (b) prohibits remote vesting by invalidating any interest not contained to vest within the specified time period. The language of EPTL 9-1.1 precludes us from adopting a "wait and see" approach to the Rule against Perpetuities. Thus, under the statute, an interest is invalid "unless it must vest, if at all, not later than 21 years after one or more lives in being." Thus, because the option in this case could have vested after the expiration of the 21 year perpetuities period, it violates the rule. We thus conclude that the option agreement is invalid. Lastly, we address Defendant Pergola's argument that if the option fails, the contract of sale conveying the property from Broadwest to Symphony (plaintiff) should be rescinded due to the mutual mistake of the parties. We disagree, as rescission is improper under the circumstances. While we agree that a contract entered into on mutual mistake of fact is generally subject to rescission, the mistake here is one of law not of fact. Thus, as we have already stated, rescission is inappropriate. The Rule against Perpetuities reflects the public policy of our State such that granting the defendant's requested relief would be contrary to public policy as it would compel performance of contracts that ultimately violate the rule.

C There exists no exception to New York's Rule against Perpetuities for commercial option agreements. New York's version of the Rule against Perpetuities measures exclusively by the passage of time, while the common law rule evaluates the reasonableness of the restraint based on its duration, purpose and designated method for fixing the purchase price. Affirmed.

III. CONCURRENT ESTATES

There are three major concurrent estates: joint tenancy, tenancy in common, and tenancy by the entirety.

A. Joint Tenancy

A joint tenancy is a form of co-ownership in which the tenant owners own an undivided interest in the whole estate. Each joint tenant has the right to possess the whole estate. The most significant factor of a joint tenancy is when one of the joint tenants dies; the remaining interest automatically goes to the surviving tenants. A joint tenancy interest cannot be passed to heirs. Additionally, there is no severance of the joint tenancy with the execution of a mortgage, a lease, a lien or divorce decree.

A joint tenancy is created with the four utilities of: time, title, interest and possession. If even one of the unities is lacking, the joint tenancy fails and a tenancy in common is created. Unity of time requires that all of the tenants' interests in the property vest at the same time. Unity of title requires the interest to be acquired by the same instrument. Unity of interest requires the tenants to share the exact same interest in the property (e.g., duration). Also, all of the tenants must have a right to occupy the entire estate.

Although traditional law presumes a transfer of property to A and B is a joint tenancy, joint tenancy estates are not preferred by the courts today. Therefore, express words are needed to create such an interest. For example, words such as "To A and B as joint tenants with the right of survivorship" or "To A and B as joint tenants," create a joint tenancy.

A joint tenancy can be terminated by a sale, partition or a mortgage of the property. With respect to mortgaging the property, under a **lien theory,** a mortgage by one tenant on the property does not sever the tenancy. However in a **title**

theory jurisdiction, a mortgage by one tenant does sever the tenancy.

B. Tenancy in Common

A tenancy in common is a concurrent ownership where each tenant owns a separate share of the property but has an equal right to possess the whole regardless of the actual share owned. This type of ownership has no right of survivorship and each tenant may pass his interest in the property (e.g., the property is freely alienable).

A tenancy in common is created by default. However, a tenancy in common is terminated by the ouster of a tenant, merger of tenant's interests, death of a tenant or partition of the property.

C. Tenancy by the Entirety

A tenancy by the entirety is a co-ownership of property similar to a joint tenancy but solely based on husband and wife ownership. A tenancy by the entirety is created using the same four utilities for a joint tenancy (time, title, interest and possession), with the additional utility of a valid marriage between husband and wife. A tenancy by the entirety can be terminated by a transfer of the property, death of a spouse or divorce. If both husband and wife intend to transfer the interest, then the transfer is valid. If only one spouse attempts to terminate the interest, the termination will be held invalid. The death of a spouse turns the interest in the property into a fee simple in the surviving spouse. A valid divorce decree severs a tenancy by the entirety, creating a joint tenancy in one person or a tenancy in common.

ESTATE	DEFINATION	CREATION	TERMINATION
Joint Tenancy	Tenancy acquired by two or more persons with the right of survivorship.	Four Utilities: • Time • Title • Interest • Possession	• Sale • Partition • Mortgage
Tenancy in Common	Property owned concurrently by two or more persons with a right to possess the whole with no right of survivorship.	Default tenancy.	• Ouster • Merger • Death • Partition
Tenancy by the Entirety	Property held between husband and wife.	Four utilities and a valid marriage.	• Transfer • Death • Divorce

SEVERENCE OF JOINT TENANCIES

Riddle v. Harmon

(1980) 102 Cal. App. 3d 525, 162 Cal. Rptr. 530

FACTS

Mr. and Mrs. Riddle purchased a parcel of real estate, taking title as joint tenants. Several months before her death, Mrs. Riddle retained an attorney to plan her estate. After reviewing the pertinent documents, he advised her that the property was held in joint tenancy and that, upon her death, the property would pass to her husband. Distressed upon learning this, she requested that the joint tenancy be terminated so that she could dispose of her property interest by will. As result, the attorney prepared a Grant Deed whereby Mrs. Riddle granted to herself an undivided ½ interest in the subject property. The document also provided that "the purpose of this grant deed is to terminate those joint tendencies formally existing between the Grantor, Francis P. Riddle and Jack C. Riddle, her husband." He also prepared the will disposing of Mrs. Riddle's interest in the property. Both the Grant Deed and the will were executed on December 8, 1975. Mrs. Riddle died 20 days later. The lower court refused to sanction her plan to sever the joint tenancy and quieted title to the property in her husband. The executrix of the will of Frances Riddle (defendant) appeals from that judgment.

I Can a joint tenant unilaterally terminate (sever) a joint tenancy by conveying her interest from herself as joint tenant to herself as tenant in common?

R A joint tenancy can be severed unilaterally by a joint tenant without the use of an intermediate third party (e.g., a "strawman") by conveying his interest in the property to himself.

A A joint tenancy can be severed unilaterally by a joint tenant without the use of an intermediate third party (e.g., a "strawman") by conveying the joint tenant's interest in the property to himself. In *Clark v. Carter* (transfer of property requires two parties, a grantor and a grantee) the wife's action of conveying her interest to herself was found not to sever the joint tenancy. In that case, the Court of Appeal found the "strawman" to be an essential part of a valid and successful conveyance. The law of requiring two separate participants to transfer property was rooted in the English common-law ceremony of livery of seisin. However, in the instant case, we abandon that antiquated rule that one cannot convey an interest in property to oneself. Similarly, we reject the logic of *Clark* because the English common law ceremony of livery of seisin as the means of transferring of title has been replaced in modern times with grant deeds and title companies. Moreover, with the passage of time and the development of new caselaw, several legal tools have been created to circumvent *Clark* thus undercutting the rule. Judgment of the lower court is reversed.

C Yes. A joint tenancy can be severed unilaterally by a joint tenant without the use of an intermediate third party (e.g., a "strawman") by conveying the joint tenant's interest in the property to himself.

Harms v. Sprague

(1984) 105 Ill. 2d 215, 473 N.E. 2d 930

FACTS

On June 26, 1973, Plaintiff William Harms and his brother, John Harms, held title to real estate (Property No. 1) as joint tenants with full survivorship rights. In a separate transaction years later, Defendant Charles Sprague, the future executor of the estate of John Harms, negotiated to purchase some property (Property No. 2) from the Simmonses (co-defendants) for $25,000. The Simmonses requested that Sprague sign a promissory note for $7,000 before finalizing the sale. So on June 12, 1981, John Harms and Charles Sprague executed a promissory note for $7,000 payable to the Simmonses. The note stated that it was to be paid by the future proceeds of the sale of John Harms's ½ interest in Property No. 1, not later than six months from the date the note was signed. However, John Harms also executed a mortgage, in favor of the Simmonses, on his undivided ½ interest in Property No. 1 to secure the payment of the same note. Plaintiff and co-tenant William Harmes was unaware of the mortgage. On December 10, 1981, John Harms died and devised his entire estate to Defendant Sprague. The mortgage from John Harms to the Simmonses was recorded on December 29, 1981. The trial court held that the mortgage severed the joint tenancy and survived John Harms's death. The Appellate Court reversed and found the property unencumbered by the mortgage.

I (1) Is a joint tenancy severed when less than all of the joint tenants mortgage their interest in the property? (2) Does the mortgage survive the death of the mortgagor and become a lien on the property (borrower or debtor)?

R A mortgage does not sever a joint tenancy in a lien theory jurisdiction and the surviving joint tenant takes an interest of a deceased joint tenant without being encumbered by the mortgage.

A A lien on a joint tenant's interest in property does not sever the joint tenancy in a lien theory jurisdiction, absent the conveyance by deed following the repayment of a mortgage debt. We find support for this position in both *Peoples Trust and Savings Bank v. Haas* (judgment lien secured against one tenant did not sever the joint tenancy) and *Van Antwerp v. Horan* (levy upon interest of a debtor joint tenant does not destroy unity of interest and does not sever the joint tenancy). This is because the mortgage title only exists between the mortgagee (lender) and the mortgagor (borrower) so title does not transfer between them. Thus, the mortgage executed by John Harms does not survive as a lien on plaintiff's property. A surviving joint tenant succeeds to the share of the deceased joint tenant by virtue of the conveyance which created the joint tenancy, not as the successor of the deceased. The property right of the mortgaging joint tenant is extinguished at the moment of his death. While John Harms was alive, the mortgage existed as a lien on his interest in the joint tenancy. Upon his death, the interest ceased to exist in along with it the lien of the mortgage.

C A mortgage does not sever a joint tenancy in a lien theory jurisdiction and the surviving joint tenant takes an interest of a deceased joint tenant without being encumbered by the mortgage. Judgment affirmed.

RELATIONS AMONG CONCURRENT OWNERS: PARTITION

Delfino v. Vealencis

(1980) 181 Conn. 533, 436 A.2d 27

FACTS

Plaintiffs Angelo and William Delfino and Defendant Helen Vealencis own real property as tenants in common. The property is a rectangular 20.5 acre parcel of land with defendant's house on the extreme western side of it. The Delfinos own an undivided 99/144 interest in the land, and defendants own a 45/144 interest. The defendants and the plaintiffs are the sole owners of the property. Defendant also runs a rubbish and garbage removal business on a portion of the land. None of the parties present, however, are in actual possession of the remainder of the property. Plaintiffs, one of whom is a residential developer, want to develop the property into 45 residential lots. So in 1978, plaintiffs brought an action in the trial court seeking a partition of the property by sale with the proceeds of the sale divided according to their respective interests. Defendant moved for judgment of in-kind partition (court ordered physical partition of the land). After a hearing, the trial court concluded that a partition in kind would result in "material injury" to both parties. The court then ordered the property to be sold at auction by a committee, and that the proceeds be paid into the court for distribution to the respective parties.

I Did the Superior Court properly order the partition sale of property owned by the plaintiffs and the defendant as tenants in common when a physical partition is possible and that type of sale would protect the interests of only one party: the owner of a larger share of the property?

R A partition by sale should only be ordered when a physical partition of the property is impracticable or inequitable and the interests of all of the owners would be promoted by a partition by sale.

A Our courts are not required to order a physical partition of land pursuant to General Statutes §52-500 (statute governing sale of real or personal property owned by two more persons in Connecticut) and such a sale should only be ordered when a physical partition of the land is impracticable or inequitable, and when the interest of all the parties would be best served by such sale. Here, the property is basically rectangular in shape. The defendant's home is located on the far western end of it and there are two opposing ownership interests at work. While the facts demonstrate that the physical partition of the property into two separate tracks is clearly feasible, the lower courts failed to consider that a partition by sale would force the defendants to surrender their home and business, both of which were located on the property. Defendant has been in actual and exclusive possession of the property for a time and while his business might adversely affect plaintiffs' attempts to develop their residential lots, we must consider the interests of all the parties, not just the plaintiffs'. The potential economic gain for one tenant or group of tenants alone cannot justify a partition by sale. Thus, the trial court erred in ordering a partition by sale. Judgment set aside and the case is remanded.

C A partition by sale should only be ordered when a physical partition of the property is impracticable or inequitable and the interests of all of the parties would be promoted by a partition by sale.

SHARING THE BENEFITS & BURDENS OF CO-OWNERSHIP

Spiller v. Mackereth

(1976) 334 So. 2d 859

FACTS

Plaintiff John Spiller and Defendant Hettie Mackereth owned a building in Tuscaloosa, Alabama as tenants in common. The lessee, Auto-Rite, was renting the building but later vacated. Thereafter, Plaintiff Spiller began using the structure as a warehouse and acquired new locks to secure the merchandise he stored inside. Defendant then wrote a letter, dated November 15, 1973, demanding that plaintiff either vacate half of the building or pay half the rental value. When plaintiff did neither, defendant brought suit. The trial court awarded defendant $2100 in rent. Plaintiff appealed.

I Is a cotenant in possession of property liable to other cotenants for rent when there is no evidence of ouster?

R Unless otherwise agreed upon, one tenant in possession of property is not liable to his fellow tenants for the value of his use and occupation of the property unless there is ouster.

A The general rule is that an absence of an agreement to pay rent or ouster of a cotenant, one cotenant in possession is not liable to his other cotenants for the value of the use and occupation of the property. Ouster can refer to either to the beginning of the running of the statute of limitations for adverse possession or liability of an occupying tenant for rent to other cotenants. The Alabama cases involving as adverse possession require a finding that the possessing cotenant asserted complete ownership of the land to support a conclusion of ouster. The finding of assertion of ownership may be established in several ways. The instant case involves a cotenant's liability for rent. Indeed, the adverse possession rule is precluded in this case by Spiller's acknowledgment of the cotenancy relationship, as evidenced by the filing of the bill for partition. We now turn to the issue of rent liability. Before an occupying cotenant can be liable for rent in Alabama, he must have denied his cotenant the right to enter. Simply requesting the occupying cotenant to vacate is not sufficient because the occupying cotenant holds title to the whole and may rightfully occupy the whole unless the other cotenants assert their possessory rights. In the instant case, defendant's letter demanded only that plaintiff vacate or pay rent but did not indicate any desire to enter the building. Defendant argues that plaintiff's installation of new locks is clear proof of an ouster. Yet the evidence does not support the fact that the locks were used for any purpose other than to secure plaintiff's goods inside. Similarly, there is no evidence to suggest that defendant or any other cotenant was barred from entering the building because of the locks. Thus, without evidence of an ouster, plaintiff is not liable for rent.

C Unless otherwise agreed upon, one tenant in possession of property is not liable to his fellow tenants for the value of his use and occupation of the property unless there is ouster. Reversed.

Swartzbaugh v. Sampson

(1936) 11 Cal. App. 2d 451, 54 P. 2d 73

FACTS

Mrs. Schwartzbaugh brings action against her husband and Defendant Sampson to cancel two leases. The Schwartzbaughs owned 60 acres of land bearing walnut trees as joint tenants with survivorship rights. In 1933, Defendant Sampson negotiated with the Schwartzbaughs to lease a portion of their land in order to build a boxing pavilion. Plaintiff Mrs. Schwartzbaugh sternly objected to his proposal. Nevertheless, on January 5, 1934, a lease option was executed by Sampson and Mr. Schwartzbaugh. The lease itself was executed by the two on February 2, 1934, with a second lease for property adjoining the boxing pavilion site also signed. Plaintiff refused to sign the documents and her name does not appear on any of them. The walnut trees were cut down and removed from the leased area. Defendant took possession, built his pavilion and made improvements to the property. This action was commenced on June 20, 1934. Plaintiff received no part of the rental income from the leased property and claimed that she never wanted the arena on her land because of the immoral and illicit activity that came with it. A nonsuit was filed by the defendant and the motion was granted. Plaintiff appealed.

I Can one joint tenant, who has not joined in the leases executed by a cotenant, maintain an action to cancel the leases where the lessee is in exclusive possession of the leased property?

R A joint tenant has the right to convey or mortgage his or her interest in the property, even if the other joint tenant objects.

A Each joint tenant in a joint tenancy owns an equal interest in and has an equal right to possession of the entire property. Each joint tenant, during the existence of the joint estate, has the right to convey, mortgage or subject to a mechanic's lien an equal share of the joint property. Also, one joint tenant in possession of the property may pledge his interest in the property to another. The pledgee's rights are valid to the extent of the pledge or his interest and each joint tenant has an equal right of possession. The pledgee has the same right of possession that the pledgor had and the joint tenant out of possession can maintain no action against the pledgee that he could not maintain against the pledgor. Thus, the lease was a valid contract entitling both Mr. Schwartzbaugh and Sampson to the same right of possession to the same leased property. Sampson has, in effect, the same rights to the leased property that Mrs. Schwartzbaugh had prior to the lease and she cannot cancel the leases because a joint tenant cannot recover exclusive possession of joint property from a cotenant absent an ouster. Plaintiff may fear that she may lose her interest in the premises by prescription but this reasoning is unfounded because a lessee cannot generally dispute a landlord's title or claim adverse possession while retaining the property under lease conditions.

C A joint tenant has the right to convey or mortgage his or her interest in the property, even if the other joint tenant objects. Judgment affirmed.

MARTIAL INTERESTS: DURING MARRIAGE

Sawada v. Endo

(1977) 57 Hawaii 608, 561 P.2d 1291

FACTS

Husband and wife Kokichi (defendant) and Ume Endo owned real property in Hawaii as tenants by the entirety. In November 1968, Plaintiffs-Appellants Masako and Helen Sawada were injured in an auto accident by a car driven by the defendant. Helen filed a complaint against defendant for damages on June 17, 1969. Thereafter, the Endos conveyed their property to their sons by deed on July 26, 1969. Plaintiff filed suit against defendant on August 13, 1969, and the complaint and summons was served on defendant on October 29, 1969. On December 17, 1969, the deed from the Endos to their sons was recorded. Neither son paid consideration for the conveyance and were aware at the time of the conveyance that their father had been in an accident and carried no liability insurance. The Endos continued to live on the property they deeded to their sons. A judgment was entered in favor of Helen Sawada for $8,846.46 and Kokichi Swada for $16,199.20 on January 19, 1971. Ume Endo died on January 29, 1971 and was survived by her husband, Kokichi. Plaintiffs-Appellants brought suit to satisfy their judgment by setting aside the deeded property. The trial court refused and the plaintiffs appealed.

I Is the interest of one spouse in real property subject to levy and execution by his or her creditors if held as a tenancy by the entirety?

R Since neither spouse acting alone can transfer his or her interest, a Tenancy by the Entirety is not subject to the claims of creditors of only one spouse.

A Today, we join a group of states including the District of Columbia which hold that under the Married Women's Property Act the interest of the husband or wife in an estate by the entirety is not subject to the claims of his or her individual creditors during the joint lives of the spouses. Spouses who hold property as Tenants by the Entirety are each considered to take the whole estate, such that each spouse enjoys all the privileges that the ownership offers. However, neither spouse has a separate divisible interest in the property that can be conveyed or reached by the execution of a judgment. While a joint tenancy may be severed by such a process, a Tenancy by the Entirety cannot. Thus, this type of estate is not divisible, and this is the critical feature of the Tenancy by the Entirety. It can only be created by a married couple, and hence can only be destroyed at the actions of a married couple. However, there is nothing to prevent a creditor from in insisting that the property held as a tendency by the entirety be subject to levy <u>before</u> extending credit.

C No. Since neither spouse acting alone can transfer his or her interest, a Tenancy by the Entirety is not subject to the claims of creditors of only one spouse.

United States v. 1500 Lincoln Avenue

949 F.2d 73 (3rd. Cir. 1991)

FACTS

Defendant A. Leonard Bernstein, and his wife, Linda Bernstein, owned property on 1500 Lincoln Avenue, the site of Pentown Pharmacy Inc., in Pittsburgh, Pennsylvania. From 1984 to 1987, Leonard used the property for the illegal distribution of prescription drugs. Thereafter, he was indicted for 51 related offenses by a federal grand jury, pled guilty and was convicted. Under 21 U.S.C. §81 (property used in furtherance of a drug crime is to be forfeited unless the owner had no knowledge of the crime or gave no consent), the Government filed a civil forfeiture complaint for the property and the pharmacy. In her answer to the complaint, Linda Bernstein averred that she had no knowledge of the illegal activity and successfully raised "a valid innocent owner defense." The Government agreed, acknowledging that Leonard's illegal activities severed the estate by the entirety and that Mrs. Bernstein was thus entitled to keep a ½ interest in the property. The District Court dismissed the complaint and the Government moved to amend. That motion was denied, but the court noted that the Government could file a *lis pendens* (notice that loss was pending against the property in question) against the property to preserve its ability to seek forfeiture of defendant's interest in the event Leonard's wife predeceased him or the tenancy was severed. The Government appealed.

I Can one Tenant by the Entirety extinguish the rights of the other tenant by subjecting the property to forfeiture?

R One Tenant by the Entirety cannot extinguish the rights of the other tenant by subjecting the property to forfeiture because each tenant has an equal right to possess/use the whole property during his lifetime, an equal right to obtain title in fee simple absolute if his cotenant predeceases him and is protected against any levy on the property by any of the cotenant's creditors.

A 21 U.S.C. §881 was intended to promote (1) the forfeiture of property used in committing drug offenses, and (2) the protection of property rights of innocent owners. Here, Mrs. Bernstein was an innocent owner and held title as a Tenant by the Entirety. Thus, she has the right to possess and use the whole property during her entire life; the right to acquire title in fee simple absolute should her husband predecease her and is protected against any lien upon her husband's former interest including any act to compel her to surrender title without her assent. We reject the lower court's plan to use a *lis pendens* as it would frustrate the innocent owner's property rights and complicate forfeiture proceedings by forcing the government to wait until Mrs. Bernstein acquires an interest in the property. This may take years to happen, leading to evidentiary problems. Thus, the District Court should first establish whether Mr. Bernstein's interest is even subject to forfeiture and, if it is, then it should be forfeited; however, defendant's interest should nonetheless be preserved.

C A Tenant by the Entirety has the right to possess/use the whole property during his lifetime and is protected against any levy on the property by any of the cotenant's creditors. Case remanded.

MARTIAL INTERESTS: TERMINATION BY DIVORCE

In re Marriage of Graham
(1978) 574 P.2d 75

FACTS

Plaintiff-Petitioner Anne Graham and her husband Dennis were married for six years. During that time, Anne was employed full-time as an airline stewardess. Defendant- Respondent Dennis Graham worked part-time for most of the marriage, devoting his time to his education. Defendant attended school for about 3 ½ years during the marriage, acquiring a BS in engineering physics and M.B.A. Following graduation, he obtained a corporate position at a starting salary of $14,000 a year.

During the marriage, plaintiff sustained roughly 70% of the financial burden, which was used for family expenses and for her husband's education. The couple accumulated no marital assets during the marriage. Plaintiff did the majority of the cooking and housework. No children were born during the marriage. Both parties filed jointly for divorce on February 4, 1974. Petitioner made no claim for support or attorney fees. The trial court ruled that that an education degree acquired by one spouse during the marriage is property jointly owned to which the other spouse has a claim. The future earnings value of the M.B.A. to respondent was valued at $82,836 and plaintiff was awarded $33,134 of that amount. The Court of Appeals reversed.

I Does a person's graduate degree (M.B.A.) constitute property which can be divided between spouses in the event of a divorce?

R An educational degree is not considered jointly owned property and is thus not subject to partition upon divorce.

A The purpose of the division of marital property is to give each spouse to property that fairly belongs to him or her. As the court in *Carlson v. Carlson* held, there is no rigid formula that the court must follow in dividing such assets. Our legislature has intended the term "property" to be broadly inclusive, as indicated by the qualifying adjective "all" in section 14-10-113(2) of the Colorado code. However, there are limits on what actually constitutes property. An educational degree is not included by even a broad reading of the concept of "property." This is because an educational degree is personal to the holder and the degree itself terminates upon the death of the holder. Furthermore, it is not inheritable. It cannot be assigned, sold, transferred, conveyed or pledged. Viewed in its most basic form, the degree is simply an intellectual achievement that may assist in the future acquisition of property, but is not considered property in and of itself. However, when one spouse provides the financial support during which time the other spouse obtains an educational degree, that contribution will taken into account when the marital property is divided. In this case, though, no marital property has been amassed by the Grahams.

C No. An educational degree is not considered jointly owned property and is thus not subject to partition upon divorce. Judgment affirmed.

Elkus v. Elkus

(1991) 169 A.D.2d 134, 572 N.Y.S.2d 901

FACTS

Plaintiff Frederica von Stade Elkus, moved for a determination, prior to trial, as to whether her career and/or celebrity status constituted marital property subject to equitable distribution. When she and her husband (defendant), a singer and teacher, were married on February 9, 1973, plaintiff was a beginning opera singer. Plaintiff achieved remarkable success during the marriage in that endeavor. Her income went from $2,250 in 1973 to $621,878 in 1989. She became internationally known, won numerous awards and performed for the President of the United States. Defendant traveled with her throughout the world during their marriage, attending, evaluating and appraising her performances and rehearsals, photographing her for magazine articles and served as her voice coach and teacher. During their 10 years of the marriage he also took care of their two children. In order to devote his time to her success and to the children, defendant claimed that he sacrificed his own career as a singer and teacher. Plaintiff claims her career and superstar status are the products of her talent and are unlicensed, and thus do not constitute property. Defendant claims that because the plaintiff's status as an opera singer increased in value in part because of his efforts, he is thus entitled to an equitable distribution of the value of her career, as measured by her earning power, as marital property. The New York Supreme Court rejected his argument and he appealed.

I When the efforts of one spouse increase the value of the other spouse's career, does that increase in value constitutes martial property subject to equitable distribution?

R The nature and extent of the contribution by the spouse seeking equitable distribution, rather than the nature of the career (whether licensed or not) of the other spouse is what determines the status of the undertaking as marital property; thus, when the efforts of one spouse increase the value of the other spouse's career, that increase in value constitutes martial property subject to equitable distribution.

A Things of value that are acquired during a marriage are marital property, even if they do not fit the traditional property concepts, *O'Brien v. O'Brien* (marital licensed constitutes marital property because it increases one's earning capacity). The *O'Brien* court also cited New York Domestic Relations Law §236 in its decision which states that "when making an equitable distribution of marital property, the court shall consider any direct or indirect contribution a spouse makes "to the career or career potential of the other spouse." Thus, the property may be either tangible or intangible and an interest in one's career counts as marital property. Examples of contributions by the other spouse include both financial and non-financial contributions, such as caring for the home and/or family. The fact that plaintiff's career is not a licensed occupation like that of a lawyer or a doctor is irrelevant. This is because it is the increased earning capacity, not the actual license or degree, which constitutes marital property. In this case, the defendant definitively made direct and material assistance to plaintiff's career, and spent time caring for the children. While plaintiff's talent existed before the marriage and already held a position in the Metropolitan Opera, her career was only in the initial stages of development. During the marriage, defendant was actively involved in her career, through his critiquing, teaching, and coaching of her. Therefore, to the extent that the growth in plaintiff's career was due in part to defendant's efforts and support, this increase constitutes marital property.

C Yes. Judgment reversed.

RIGHTS OF DOMESTIC PARTNERS

Baker v. State

170 Vt. 194, 744 (1999)

FACTS

Plaintiffs are three same-sex couples who have lived together in committed relationships for periods ranging from four to 25 years. Baker is the named plaintiff representing the others in the suit. Two of the couples have raised children together. Each couple applied for a marriage license from the respective town clerk and each was refused a license as ineligible under the applicable state marriage laws. Plaintiffs thereupon filed this lawsuit against defendants, the state of Vermont, the towns of Milton and Shelburne and the City of South Burlington, seeking a declaratory judgment that the refusal to issue them a license violated the Vermont Constitution. The trial court ruled that the marriage statutes were constitutional, because they rationally furthered the state's interest in promoting "the link between procreation and child rearing." This appeal followed.

I May the State of Vermont exclude same-sex couples from the benefits and protections that its laws provide to opposite-sex couples?

R Same-sex couples are assured the same rights, benefits and protections provided to married opposite-sex couples under the Common Benefits Clause of the Vermont Constitution.

A The Common Benefits Clause of the Vermont Constitution reads that "government is, or ought to be, instituted for the common benefit, protection, and security of the people, nation or community and not for the particular emolument or advantage of any single person, family, or set of persons, who are part only of that community." Thus, we hold that the State is constitutionally required to extend same-sex couples the common benefits and protections that flow from marriage under Vermont law. Plaintiff claims that denial of a civil marriage license excludes same-sex couples from a broad array of legal benefits including spousal medical, life and disability insurance. The

State argues that the trial court did not err in upholding the law because the law reasonably serves the State's interest in promoting the "link between procreation and child rearing." We note that many states and the federal government have enacted laws prohibiting discrimination in any context on the basis of sexual orientation. We thus hold that State has not met its burden in providing a reasonable and just basis for the exclusion of same-sex couples from the benefits and protections afforded to a civil marriage. Therefore, same-sex couples are entitled to the same benefits and protections afforded by Vermont law to married opposite-sex couples, but we note that it is up to the legislature to craft an appropriate means of addressing this directive. The current system shall remain in place for a reasonable amount of time in order to allow the legislature to do so.

C No. Same-sex couples are assured the same rights, benefits and protections provided to married opposite-sex couples under the Common Benefits Clause of the Vermont Constitution. Reversed.

IV. NON-FREEHOLD ESTATES

A. Estate for Years

An estate for years is an interest in property that lasts for a fixed period of time as set forth in a lease. An estate for years is terminated automatically at the expiration of the lease or upon surrender by the leaseholder.

B. Periodic Tenancy

A periodic tenancy is a tenancy for a fixed duration and continues for succeeding periods until either the landlord or the tenant gives notice of termination. If no notice is given, then the tenancy extends for another duration period.

A periodic tenancy is created by the express agreement of both parties, by implication or by operation of law. A periodic tenancy is created by implication if a lease provides for no termination date but there exist consistent payments of rent in fixed duration periods (monthly rent). A periodic tenancy is created by operation of law where the tenant holds over after the expiration of the lease term (discussed below).

A periodic tenancy is terminated with proper notice. Notice can be given orally or by writing. The notice must equal the length of the rental period except in the instance of an annual lease (only 6 months notice is required). For example, if a lease term creates week to week tenancy, notice must be given one week prior to termination.

C. Tenancy at Will

A tenancy at will is a tenancy with no stated duration, either by express terms or by operation of law. A tenancy at will continues as long as both the landlord and tenant agree to continue. If either the landlord or tenant wishes to terminate the tenancy, the tenancy is terminated. Notice is not required to terminate a tenancy at will.

D. Holdover Tenant

A holdover tenant is a tenant that continues in possession after the termination of the tenancy. Once a tenant becomes a holdover tenant, the landlord has two options: (1) allow the tenant to stay on the premises or (2) evict him. Most jurisdictions allow for a periodic tenancy to be created once the landlord consents to the tenant staying on the premises. The new period is measured by the length of the original tenancy duration and governed by the provisions of the old lease.

ESTATE	DEFINATION	CREATION	TERMINATION
Estate for Years	Tenancy for a fixed period of time	Written lease	• Expiration of lease • Surrender of lease holder
Periodic Tenancy	Tenancy for durational intervals	• Expressly • Implication • Operation of law	• Proper notice
Tenancy at Will	Tenancy with no stated duration	• Express terms • Operation of law	• By either landlord or tenant
Holdover Tenant	When a tenant holds over after the termination of the tenancy	When tenant stays past allowed duration of possession	• Creation of a periodic tenancy • Eviction

TENANCY AT WILL

Garner v. Gerrish

(1984) 63 N.Y.2d 575; 473 N.E.2d 2

FACTS

In 1977 Robert Donovan owned a house located in Potsdam, New York. On April 14, 1977 he leased the premises to a tenant, Lou Gerrish. The lease was executed on a printed form, neither party being represented by counsel. The blanks in the form were filled in by Donovan. With respect to the duration of the tenancy, the lease provided it shall continue for and during the term of quiet enjoyment from the first day of May, 1977, which term will end and Lou Garrish has the option of terminating the lease at the date of his choice. The lease also contained a standard reference to the landlord's right of reentry if the rent was not timely paid. Gerrish lived there absent any confrontation until 1981. In 1981, Donovan died and Plaintiff Garner became the executor of his estate. Thereafter, Garner called for defendant to leave the premises. Defendant refused and this action was initiated by the plaintiff. Plaintiff argues that the lease created a tendency at will because the length of the lease was indefinite. Defendant argues that the lease created a determinable life tenancy by its language.

I Does a lease which grants a tenant the right to terminate a lease create a determinable life tenancy or merely establishes a tenancy at will?

R A determinable life tenancy is created if a lessee has the option of terminating a lease when he pleases.

A At common law, the rule was that "at least for so long as the lessee shall please is a lease at will of both lessee and lessor." That is, as long as the lessee adhered to the terms of the lease and both the lessor and lessee agreed that the lease should continue, the lease was in force. This rule had its origin in the ancient ritual of livery of seisin, where the transfer of a clod of dirt, was required to create a life estate. However, because the livery of seisin, like the requirement for a seal, has been abandoned, commentators generally urge that there is no longer any reason why a lease granting the tenant alone the right to terminate at will, should be converted into a tendency at will terminable by either party. Today, however, the courts look to the terms of the agreement to determine what type of lease has been a created. In the instant case, the terms of the agreement clearly indicate that Donovan and defendant agreed that defendant would have a determinable life tenancy. As such, the lower court's judgment is reversed.

C Yes. A determinable life tenancy is created if a lessee has the option of terminating a lease when he pleases.

TENANCY AT SUFFERANCE: HOLDOVERS

Crechale & Polles, Inc. v. Smith

295 So. 2d 275 (1974)

FACTS

In 1964 Plaintiff-Appellant Crechale & Polles (lessor), a Mississippi corporation, entered into a lease with Defendant-Appellee John and Gloria Smith (lessee). The term of the lease was for five years commencing on February 7, 1964 and expiring on February 6, 1969. As the end of the lease approached, Smith learned that the new building he intended to occupy would not be readily available. Defendant notified plaintiff that he wished to hold over on a month-to-month basis. Smith contends that he was informed that he could stay until his new building was ready. Subsequently, Smith's attorney drafted a document evidencing a 30 day extension for Crechale to sign. Crechale denies it was ever given the document. Plaintiff refused the month-to-month offer and told defendant that he would have to vacate at the end of the lease. Thereafter, Smith held over. Plaintiff accepted the payment for the first month and sued to bind Smith for the full lease term. The court awarded complainants $1750.00 in back rent payments and $760 for damages. From this judgment, the appellant files this appeal.

I If a landlord hold a tenant to a new lease term after he elected to treat that same holdover tenant as a trespasser?

R After having elected not to accept the appellees as tenants, the appellant could not at a later date, after failing to pursue his remedy to evict the tenants, change the election to hold the appellees as tenants for a new term.

A We are convinced that the appellant is not entitled to require the appellees to pay rent for a new term of the rental contract as a holdover tenant. This is evidenced by the fact that after Smith confirmed an alleged agreement to extend the lease on a month-to-month basis, Crechale immediately wrote Smith and denied that there was such an agreement and demanded that Smith quit and vacate the premises at the end of the lease. Thus, the letter from the appellant was an effective election on the part of the landlord-appellant to terminate the lease and to treat the appellees as trespassers. After having elected not to accept the appellees as tenants, the appellant could not thereafter change his mind and hold the appellees as tenants for a new term. Although the appellant-landlord expressly refused to extend the lease on a month-to-month basis, nevertheless, he accepted and cashed the rent check for the month of February. The effect of this action by a landlord is tantamount to an extension of the lease for the period of time for which the check was accepted, unless, of course, the landlord had elected to treat the tenant as a holdover tenant. We hold that once a landlord elects to treat a tenant as a trespasser and refuses to extend the lease on a month-to-month basis, fails to pursue his remedy of ejecting the tenant but accepts monthly checks for rent due, he is in effect agreeing to an extension of the lease on a month-to-month basis.

C No. A landlord may not change his mind after he elects to treat a tenant as a trespasser or holds him to a new term. Judgment affirmed.

THE LEASE: UNLAWFUL DISCRIMINATION

Soules v. U.S. Dept. of Housing & Urban Develop.

967 F.2d 917 (2nd Cir. 1992)

FACTS

Plaintiff-Petitioner Sherry Soules was a single woman searching for an apartment for her 12-year-old daughter, her mother and herself in Buffalo, New York. Plaintiff responded to an advertisement by Defendant-Respondent Mary Jean Downs, a realtor. During their first telephone interview, Downs asked the plaintiff's child's age and whether she was "loud." Plaintiff became annoyed and asked why such information was needed. Downs replied that two elderly tenants living in the first-floor unit did not want an upstairs neighbor who was noisy. Thereafter, plaintiff contacted Housing Opportunities Made Equal Inc. (HOME), a nonprofit corporation that investigates alleged incidents of housing discrimination. HOME investigated the discrimination allegations by having two "testers" impersonate applicants and then record the outcome of the interaction. When contacted by the HOME testers, Downs agreed to show the apartment to the tester who had no children, but not to the tester who had a seven-year-old son. When plaintiff finally met with Downs, she was shown a less appealing apartment and told that there were no apartments in the Richmond area currently available. Afterwards, Downs showed the apartment in question to the Perry family who had children, but eventually rented it to a single woman with no children. Plaintiff and HOME brought an action under the Fair Housing Act (FHA) but an Administrative Law judge (ADL) denied plaintiffs' (Soules and HOME) claim, ruling instead that Downs did not violate the FHA. The ruling became a final order of the U.S. Department of Housing & Urban Development (HUD). Plaintiffs brought a petition for review before the Court of Appeals.

I (1) If a housing provider provides a legitimate, nondiscriminatory reason for refusing to rent to a prospective applicant, can it then defeat a rental applicant's claim of discrimination? (2) Are factfinders allowed to inquire as to a housing provider's discriminatory intent when questioning prospective renters about family status?

R By showing legitimate reasons for refusing to rent, housing providers can defeat discrimination claims; and factfinders are permitted to make inquiries as to a hosing provider's intent when questing prospective rental applicants concerning their family status.

A If a housing provider provides a legitimate, nondiscriminatory reason for refusing to rent to a prospective applicant, it can defeat a rental applicant's claim of discrimination. In this case, the plaintiff established a prima facie case of discrimination by proving that Downs denied the apartment to Soules knowing of her familial status. However, Downs asserted two legitimate reasons for denying to rent to the plaintiff: (1) Soules's hostile tone towards her and (2) the fact that Downs was frequently out of town caring for a sick aunt. As such, we agree with Respondent Downs and find that the evidence supports the Administrative Law Judge's (ALJ) conclusion that Downs had legitimate reasons for not renting to the plaintiff. Specifically, the treatment of the Perrys indicates that Downs was willing to rent to a family with children. Petition denied. (2) Yes. Factfinders are permitted to make inquiries as to a hosing provider's intent when questing prospective rental applicants about their family status. While blatant discriminatory statements violate the FHA, it is not necessarily objectionable to inquire as to whether a prospective renter has children or whether they are "loud." More exactly, it is a factual question whether such questioning has a discriminatory purpose. Therefore, it was proper for the ALJ to determine whether Downs's line of questioning was done for a legitimate purpose or was simply a pretext for discrimination. The ALJ concluded that there was no discriminatory intent or reason for asking plaintiff's daughter's age and if she was noisy. According to the ALJ's findings, Downs asked if her child was noisy in order to guarantee that the elderly tenants in the apartment below could continue to live in quiet surroundings. Her questions were not a pretext for discrimination, principally given that Downs's offered to rent to the Perrys, a family with children. Thus, we conclude that substantial evidence supported the ALJ's determination and, accordingly, the petition for review is denied.

C By showing legitimate reasons for refusing to rent, housing providers can defeat discrimination claims; and factfinders are permitted to make inquiries as to a hosing providers' intent when questing prospective rental applicants. Petition for review denied.

DELIVERY OF POSSESSION

Hannan v. Dusch

(1930) 154 Va. 356; 153 S.E. 824; 70 A.L.R. 141

FACTS

Plaintiff Hannan leased real estate from Defendant Dusch on August 31, 1927 in the city of Norfolk, Virginia, for a term of 15 years beginning January 1, 1928. At the time the lease was to commence, the tenant then in possession failed to vacate and Defendant-lessor Dusch failed to put plaintiff-lessee in possession. Plaintiff argues that the defendant has a duty to deliver him actual possession and that he should have evicted the holdover tenant. Defendant maintains that he has a duty to deliver only the legal right to possession, not actual possession. There is no covenant in the lease stating that defendant must put plaintiff in actual possession.

I Must a landlord deliver actual possession of the leased property to the tenant or just the legal right to possession?

R A landlord has a duty to deliver only the right to possession of the leased premises to a tenant, not actual possession of the property.

A We start our analysis with two rules governing this issue, absent an agreement to the contrary (e.g., a covenant): The English rule and the American rule. The English rule states that the landlord must place the tenant in possession. The American rule says that the landlord must only give the tenant the right to possession;

that is, a landlord must at least provide the legal right to possession. Moreover, once the tenant takes possession, he is responsible for ejecting a trespasser. But where a covenant exists containing a specific duty to put the tenant in possession, that covenant would prevail. In this case, however, there is no covenant in the lease, so we must choose the better rule supported by reason. We thus hold the English rule is best suited to the facts at hand for the following reasons: (1) a tenant contracts for possession and not for a lawsuit to evict a holdover; and (2) the landlord is in a better position to assess whether the current tenant will in fact, holdover. However, we choose the American rule because it is unfair to hold the landlord liable for the wrong of another. That is, under the American rule, when a new tenant fails to obtain possession of the premises because a former tenant wrongfully holds over, his remedy is against the wrongdoer and not against the landlord. This is because the landlord has not covenanted against the wrongful acts of another and should not be held responsible for such a tort unless he has expressly so contracted. This accords with the general rule as to other wrongdoers, whereas the English rule appears create a specific exception against lessors.

C A landlord has a duty to deliver only the right to possession of the leased premises to a tenant, not actual possession of the property. Judgment affirmed.

SUBLEASES & ASSIGNMENTS

Ernst v. Conditt

(1964) 54 Tenn. App. 328; 390 S.W.2d 703

FACTS

Plaintiff B. Walter Ernst and his wife leased a track land in Davidson County, Tennessee to Frank Rogers for term of one year, seven days. Rogers built and operated a racetrack as well as a Go-Cart track and improved the property by erecting floodlights. Rogers operated the business for short time and then entered into negotiations with Defendant A.K. Conditt for the sale of the business. The original lease was modified and allowed for an extension of the term of the lease by two years. Rogers was given the right to sublet the premises to Conditt on condition that Rogers remain personally liable for the performance of the terms of the lease. Thereafter, Rogers leased the premises to the defendant. In the Rogers-Conditt contract, the term "sublet" was used. After defendant took possession, he operated the racetrack for short time. Thereafter, Conditt quit paying rent, but he remained in possession. Ernst sued Condit for the rent owed. Plaintiff contends that the Rogers-Condit agreement was an assignment of the lease, thereby rendering Condit liable to Ernst. Defendant contends that the Rogers-Condit agreement was a subletting, thereby rendering Rogers directly liable to Ernst.

I How does a court determine whether an assignment or a subleasing has occurred between the respective parties?

R The determination of whether an assignment or a subleasing has occurred between the parties is based on the intentions of the parties.

A A landlord may recover from the assignee in an assignment, but not in a sublease. At common law, an assignment was created when the entire interest in a lease was conveyed and nothing was left to the original lessee. Also at common law, where the interest granted was less than that owned by the original lessee, a sublease was created and the original lessee retained a reversionary interest. Under the modern law, we look to the intention of the parties as a method of determining whether there has been an assignment or a sublease. At common law, Conditt is liable to Ernst because he took Rogers' entire interest in the land, even though the modified Rogers-Ernst contract held Rogers personally liable to Ernest. This is because Rogers's liability to Ernst is not determined by the Rogers-Conditt agreement; even though the modified Ernst-Rogers agreement contained the word "sublet." Ernest's consent to "sublet" is viewed by the court as only consent for someone other than the original lessee to go into possession. In essence, it authorizes both a subletting and an assignment. Either way, defendant is liable to plaintiff under the modern rule. Rogers retained no reversionary interest by the terms of the Rogers-Conditt agreement, as he conveyed all the rights to the property he had. Thus, Rogers has assigned is lease.

C The determination of whether an assignment or a subleasing has occurred between the parties is based on the intentions of the parties. Judgment affirmed.

Kendall v. Ernest Pestana

(1985) 40 Cal. 3d 488; 709 P.2d 837; 220 Cal. Rptr. 818

FACTS

This case concerns a commercial lease and that the lessee may not assign or sublet the premises without the lessor's prior written approval. The City of San Jose leased a 14,000 sq. ft. hanger to Irving and Janice Perlitch. Prior to assigning their interest to Defendant-Respondent Ernest Pestana, the Perlitches sublet the premises to Robert Bixler for a 25 year term to run an airplane maintenance business. Thereafter, the Perlitches assigned their interest to Defendant Ernest Pestana. Afterwards, Bixler attempted to sell his interest to Plaintiff Jack Kendall and others as the plaintiff was more financially sound than Bixler. Abiding by the terms of the original Bixler-Perlitch lease, Bixler requested consent from Pestana for the sublease. Defendant responded by demanding an increase in rent in exchange for the consent and argued that he may arbitrarily refuse consent. Plaintiff Kendall argued that Pestana's arbitrary refusal is void as against public policy because it is an unreasonable restraint on alienation.

I In the absence of a provision to the contrary, may a lessor unreasonably and arbitrarily withhold consent to an assignment?

R Only where a lessor has a commercially reasonable objection to the assignee or the proposed use may the lessor withhold consent to an assignment; such withholding of consent MAY

NOT be unreasonable or arbitrary.

A We acknowledge that the common law favors the free alienability of property; however, it may be restricted by contract as a protective measure afforded to the lessor. Traditionally, these restrictions are strictly construed against the lessor. This is particularly true when the act of assigning terminates the lease. However, this traditional majority rule has come under steady attack in recent years giving way to the following rule: a lessor may withhold consent only when he has a commercially reasonable objection to the assignee or to the assignment. Support for this modern rule can be found in the following reasoning: (1) Public policy disfavors restraints on alienation and favors free alienability; (2) the lessor's interests are protected by the fact that the original lessee remains liable to the lessor as a surety; (3) a lease is increasingly viewed as contractual in nature, such that there exist obligations imposed on both parties to deal with one another fairly and in good faith; duties which are implied by law in every contract. Thus, the lessor has discretion to withhold consent when done so in good faith and for good reason. Specifically, the lessor may withhold consent where (1) the property is not well suited for the planned use; (2) the planned use is illegal; or (3) the planned use involves an altering of the property.

C Only where a lessor has a commercially reasonable objection to the assignee or the proposed use may the lessor withhold consent to an assignment; such withholding of consent may not be unreasonable or arbitrary.

THE DEFAULTING TENANT: TENANT IN POSSESSION

Berg v. Wiley

(1978) 264 N.W.2d 145

FACTS

Defendant-landlord Wiley Enterprises Inc. and Defendant Rodney Wiley (collectively referred to hereafter as "defendant") leased land and a building to Phillip Berg for a 5 year term beginning December 1, 1970. The lease provided that no changes be made in the building structure without the defendant's consent and that defendant reserved the right to retake possession should Berg fail to meet the lease terms. Thereafter, Phillip Berg assigned the lease to Plaintiff Kathleen Berg. Without obtaining Wiley's permission, Kathleen remodeled the premises for use as a restaurant. The present dispute arose out of Wiley's objection to Kathleen's continued restaurant remodeling without his permission and her operation of it in violation of health regulations. Defendant demanded that the health code violations be remedied and that she complete the remodeling within two weeks. But after two weeks, plaintiff closed the restaurant and placed a sign on the premises that read, "Closed for Remodeling." Earlier that day, Wiley attempted to change the locks on the doors, but stopped when plaintiff arrived. Thereafter, without Plaintiff Berg's knowledge, defendant changed the locks. Berg contends that she was wrongfully evicted. Defendant raised an abandonment defense. The trial court ruled defendant's entry was forcible and this appeal was filed.

I (1) Was the evidence submitted sufficient to support the jury's finding that the tenant did not abandon or surrender the premises and (2) Did the trial court err in finding Wiley's reentry forcible and wrongful as a matter of law?

R The jury's finding is sufficient that the tenant did not abandon or surrender the premises and the trial court's determination was correct as a matter of law; thus, a landlord may NOT resort to nonpeaceable measures nor employ self-help remedies to regain possession of his land.

A A landlord may use self-help at common law if he was legally entitled to possession. Such is the case when the landlord's means of entry are peaceable and the tenant holds over. Here, defendant claims he was entitled to possession because plaintiff breached the lease. But it is for the courts, not defendant, to determine if the landlord is entitled to possession. As to whether the entry was peaceable, defendant contends that only actual or threatened use of violence should give rise to liability. We disagree. Our public policy discourages self help remedies as evidenced by both the courts and the legislature. To that end, the legislature has created summary proceedings to help landlords regain possession quickly. Thus, we find defendant's entry was not peaceable and given the sour relationship between the two parties, the only reason violence didn't erupt was because plaintiff was absent when the locks were changed. Certainly any use of self-help has violent potential. Thus, a landlord may not use self-help unless the tenant has abandoned or surrendered the premises. Else, the landlord must resort to the judicial process to regain possession.

C A landlord may not resort to nonpeaceable measures nor employ self-help remedies to regain possession of his land. Judgment affirmed.

THE TENANT WHO HAS ABANDONED POSSESSION

Sommer v. Kridel

(1977) 74 N.J. 446; 378 A.2d 767

FACTS

On March 10, 1972, Plaintiff Abraham Sommer leased apartment 6-L in the Pierre Apartments in Hackensack, N.J. to Defendant James Kridel for a two year term. Defendant paid the Sommer $690, half of which was used for the first month's rent. Prior to defendant taking possession, defendant wrote plaintiff that he could no longer afford the lease as his wedding engagement was broken and that up until that point, both sets of parents planned to take on the rent payments after the wedding. Plaintiff did not respond. Thereafter, a third party inquired about the apartment. Though the third party was ready, willing, and able to rent the apartment, she was told that it had already been rented to the defendant. After a year, the apartment was at last rented under similar terms and conditions as those negotiated with the defendant. Plaintiff sued for damages for rent due from the date defendant was to take possession until the date the apartment was finally rented to a third party. Defendant denies liability arguing that plaintiff failed to mitigate damages and because plaintiff refused to accept defendant's surrender of the premises.

I Must a landlord mitigate damages by making reasonable efforts to relet an apartment wrongfully vacated by the tenant?

R A landlord is under an affirmative duty to mitigate damages and must make reasonable efforts to relet an apartment wrongfully vacated by the tenant.

A The majority rule states that a landlord has no duty to mitigate any damages. This is because a lease is considered to be a property interest which bars any control of the property by the landlord. Thus, the reasoning goes, since a landlord has no control, it would be unrealistic to require him to mitigate. However, modern notions of fairness and equity have eroded the real property concepts which served as the basis of the majority rule and the Law of Estates has reacted by allowing specific clauses in contracts to deal with these changes. Given that we now consider a lease for the most part as a contract, we can now apply the contract principle that the landlord must mitigate damages. The basis of this rule stems from notions of fairness. That is, it would be inherently unfair to allow a landlord to simply sit by and watch damages grow when he is in a position to prevent those damages. Thus, where the landlord has many vacant apartments, he must make reasonable efforts to relet each one as applicable to the situation. Since the landlord is in the better position to prove that his efforts were reasonable, he shall have the burden of showing that his efforts were, in fact, reasonable.

C A landlord is under an affirmative duty to mitigate damages and must make reasonable efforts to relet an apartment wrongfully vacated by the tenant. Judgment reversed.

V. LANDLORD AND TENANT DUTIES

A. Landlord Duties

1. Duty to Deliver Possession

Under the common law, a landlord impliedly warrants that the tenant will have a legal right to possess of the premises. However, under the modern view, a landlord does not have an obligation to deliver possession of the premises.

2. Quiet Enjoyment

Every lease has an implied covenant of quiet enjoyment. An eviction of a tenant by a landlord breaches this covenant. There are two types of evictions, actual and constructive. Actual eviction occurs when the landlord excludes the tenant from the leased premises. Constructive eviction arises from the negligent conduct of the landlord that makes the leased premises uninhabitable.

3. Suitable Premises

A landlord is not liable for dangerous conditions existing on the leased premises. However, he may be liable in tort to the tenant, his guests, licensees, or invitees if, at the commencement of the lease, there existed a latent defect (dangerous condition) the landlord knew of or should have known about and it was not likely to be discovered by the tenant upon her reasonable inspection.

4. Duty to Repair

Under common law, absent a statute to the contrary, the landlord has no duty to maintain the leased premises. However, if the landlord does undertake a repair on the premises and does so negligently he is liable in tort for any injuries.

B. Tenant Duties

1. Duty to Pay Rent

A tenant has the duty to pay rent to the landlord for the leased premises.

2. Duty to Repair

A tenant has a duty to make ordinary repairs and maintain the leased premises.

3. Duty not to commit Waste

A tenant may not commit ameliorative waste on the leased premises. Ameliorative waste is changing the physical characteristics of the premises. This includes improvements to the leased premises which increase the value of the land/premises.

C. Fixtures

A fixture is a chattel that becomes real property because it has been permanently attached to the leased premises and may not be removed by the tenant. However, if the fixture is a trade fixture, it is removable by the tenant. A trade fixture is a fixture installed for a particular business purpose. Modern law, on the other hand, allows for all fixtures to be removed as long as the premises can be returned to its former condition.

D. Assignments and Subleases

1. Assignments

An assignment occurs when a tenant transfers the entire term of a lease and retains no interest in the lease. The original tenant is no longer in privity of estate but remains in privity of contract with the landlord. Therefore, if the assignee fails to pay his rent, the landlord may recover against the original tenant. However, if the assignee assumes all of the promises in the original lease, there is privity of contract between the landlord and assignee, and the original tenant is not liable for any non-payment of rent.

- T1 (Original Tenant) transfers whole lease to T2 (Second Tenant).
- L (Landlord) and T2 are in privity of estate and liable to each other.
- L and T2 are NOT in privity of contract unless T2 expressly assumes all promises of the original lease.

2. Subleases

A sublease occurs when a tenant transfers <u>less than</u> the entire leasehold. The tenant remains in both privity of estate and privity of contract with the landlord. In this situation, the sublessee has created no legal relationship between the landlord and himself and is therefore not liable to pay rent to the landlord.

- T1 (Original Tenant) transfers part of the lease to T2 (Sublessee).
- L and T2 share no nexus and are not in privity of estate or contract.

3. Covenants against Assignments or Subleases

Some leases contain provisions that forbid assignments or subleases without the consent of the landlord. Such provisions are strictly construed against the landlord and are usually invalid.

QUIET ENJOYMENT & CONSTRUCTIVE EVICTION

Reste Realty Corp. v. Cooper
(1969) 53 N.J. 44; 251 A.2d 268

FACTS

Defendant-lessee Joy M. Cooper leased the basement of a commercial office building from Plaintiff-lessor Reste Realty Corporation's predecessor in title on May 13, 1958. Unfortunately, whenever it would rain, water ran off an improperly surfaced driveway into her rented offices and meeting rooms below. When the basement flooded, Arthur A. Donigian, a lawyer and resident manager of the complex would quickly take steps to remove it. After a new five lease was negotiated, Donigian promised to remedy the flooding permanently. The driveway was resurfaced, but the flooding persisted. Donigian died in 1961. Thereafter, whenever it rained, defendant's complaints were ignored and it became almost impossible for her to hold her meetings there. Soon after, she vacated the premises. Plaintiff sued for the balance of the lease and argued that Cooper's abandonment was unjustified because the flooding was not permanent and because the defendant inspected the premises and nonetheless accepted the premises as is.

I If a tenant's right to quiet enjoyment is interfered with by the landlord, may the tenant vacate the premises and terminate the lease without incurring liability on the remaining lease?

R If a tenant's right to quiet enjoyment is interfered with by the landlord, he may vacate the premises and terminate the lease.

A Plaintiff-lessor Reste Realty initially argues that abandonment was unjustified because defendant inspected the premises and accepted the premises as is. We find this argument unconvincing as the faulty driveway surfacing caused the flooding and it was not part of the premises leased. Even so, we find no evidence supporting the fact that defendant knew of the defect prior to leasing her offices. Plaintiff next argues that defendant waived her right to quiet enjoyment because she released the space for another 5 year term knowing that the flood problem existed. We find this argument equally unpersuasive as Donigian promised to remedy the flooding but didn't. Thus, the key question here is whether defendant was justified in vacating. A covenant of quiet enjoyment is implied in every lease such that when a duty to act or failure act renders the site unsuitable for the leased purposes, the covenant is breached. If a breach occurs, the tenant's remedies include termination of the lease or vacating the premises. Here, Cooper could not use the basement for conducting business. This was the use for which the premises were rented. Thus, she was justified in vacating and canceling the lease. Lastly, plaintiff argues that defendant waived the right to cancel the lease because she remained in possession for an unreasonable time after learning of the defect. We disagree and hold that there was sufficient evidence for the trial court to conclude that she acted reasonably under the circumstances.

C If a tenant's right to quiet enjoyment is interfered with by the landlord, he may vacate the premises and terminate the lease. Judgment reversed.

THE IMPLIED WARRANTY OF HABITABILITY

Hilder v. St. Peter

(1984) 144 Vt. 150; 478 A.2d 202

FACTS

In October, 1974, Plaintiff Hilder and her three children rented an apartment from Defendant Stuart St. Peter for $140 per month. Plaintiff discovered a number of problems with the dwelling after taking possession and after paying the rent. There was a broken kitchen window which the defendant promised to repair but never did so. Plaintiff repaired the window at her own expense out of concern that one of her children might get cut on the glass shards. The key to the door was missing. The toilet was clogged and was filled with feces; it would only flush of water was poured down. The bathroom light and wall outlet were inoperable so outlets in adjoining rooms were used with an extension cord. Water leaked into the apartment from the upstairs apartment causing ceiling plaster to fall onto her bed and into her grandson's crib. There was also a strong odor of raw sewage in the apartment. Defendant promised to remedy all, but never did. The trial court held the Warranty of Habitability was breached and awarded plaintiff the total rent paid. Defendant argued that because plaintiff never vacated, the full award was in error. Plaintiff argues that an abandonment of the premises is not necessary.

I Does every residential lease contain an implied warranty of habitability?

R Every residential lease contains an implied warranty of habitability.

A Historically, the lessee took possession of the leased premises "as is." The landlord was under no affirmative duty to make the premises livable unless the lease contained an express covenant. Now, modern law requires that the leased land be safe, habitable and sanitary. This change can be seen as a measurement of how much society has changed. The typical tenant of the middle ages was a farmer who was capable of making repairs himself. However, today's tenant is generally unable to repair his own living unit. Therefore, in step with modern society, we now hold that there exists in every residential lease an implied covenant of habitability whose protections cannot be waived. In making a determination as to whether the warranty has been breached, courts may look to the local municipal housing codes or to the minimum state housing code standards. If the warranty is breached, the tenant must notify the landlord and allow him time to remedy the defect. If the defect is not remedied, the tenant may pursue rescission, reformation and damages; punitive or otherwise. Damages are calculated as the difference between the value of the dwelling as warranted and the value of the dwelling as defective.

Alternatively, the tenant may repair the defect and deduct the expenses from the rent or withhold the rent until damages are calculated.

C Every residential lease contains an implied warranty of habitability. Judgment affirmed in part and remitted for a calculation of damages.

THE PROBLEM OF AFFORDABLE HOUSING

Chicago Board of Realtors v. City of Chicago

819 F.2d 732 (7th Cir. 1987)

FACTS

In 1986, Chicago enacted the Residential Landlord and Tenant Ordinance, which essentially codified the implied warranty of habitability and established new landlord responsibilities and tenant rights, including the following: (1) the landlord must pay interest on security deposits; (2) the security deposit must be held in an Illinois bank; (3) a tenant may withhold rent in an amount reflecting the cost to him of the landlord's violating a term of the lease; (4) a landlord is forbidden from charging more than $10 per month for late rent; and (5) creates a rebuttable presumption that a landlord who seeks to evict a tenant after the tenant has exercised rights conferred by the ordinance is retaliating against the tenant for the exercise of those rights. The district court denied a motion for a preliminary injunction brought by the group of property owners (Chicago Board of Realtors) challenging the constitutionality of the ordinance as violative of the Contracts Cause the Constitution, violating Procedural and Substantive Due Process, the Equal Protection Clause and that is was void for vagueness. We now hear the plaintiffs' appeal.

I Is a rent control ordinance that is sufficiently specific reasonable in light of its stated purpose to promote public health, safety and welfare?

R A rent control ordinance which is sufficiently specific and gives due deference to the legislative judgment is reasonable in light of its stated purpose to promote public health, safety and welfare.

A We start by noting that our interest here is not the constitutional analysis of the issues presented but rather a policy analysis. We agree that the ordinance is reasonable, but we acknowledge a strong argument to the contrary because it reapportions landlord and tenant rights. While the ordinance was designed to promote social welfare, its real intention is debatable. Additionally, its actual impact is doubtful because landlords will most likely try to raise rents if they cannot charge more than $10 for late rent; and if tenants can withhold rent, landlords will not improve housing as it will no longer pay. This will ultimately hurt tenants and force those who cannot pay higher rents to go homeless. If the landlords can't raise rents, more resources will go to condominiums, reducing the net stock of housing. The state bank provision of the ordinance requiring security deposits to be placed in Illinois banks serves as a wealth transfer tool promoting class legislation and protectionism and benefiting the middle class, not the poor. Essentially, this ordinance transfers wealth from out-of-state banks and tenants to the middle class allowing the middle class to get preferential treatment by the landlords because they are a better risk against late rent. This becomes apparent once one understands that out-of-state persons can't vote in Chicago state and local elections and those with very low incomes generally don't vote.

C A rent control ordinance which apportions tenant-landlord rights is reasonably related to a legitimate public goal.

VI. EASEMENTS

An easement is the right of a person to go onto the land of another to make limited use of the property.

A. Easement Classifications

1. Easement Appurtenant

An easement appurtenant is an easement created to benefit another tract of land, the use of which is incident to the ownership of the land. There are two parcels of land that are involved in an easement appurtenant; the dominant estate and servient estate. The dominant estate is the land whose owner is benefited by the easement. The servient estate is the land that is burdened by the easement.

2. Easement in Gross

An easement is gross is an easement benefiting a particular person and not a particular piece of land. For example, A's use of a billboard on B's land is an easement in gross because the billboard is benefiting A and not B's land.

3. Affirmative Easements

An affirmative easement is an easement that forces the owner of the servient estate to permit certain actions by the easement holder. For example, if A is permitted to discharge water onto B's servient estate, there is an affirmative easement.

4. Negative Easements

A negative easement is an easement that prohibits the owner of the servient estate from doing something. For example, if A is prohibited from building a structure that obstructs the view of B's building, a negative easement is present.

B. Creating an Easement

1. Creation by Express Grant

Easements are subject to the statute of frauds and therefore must be in writing and signed by the party charged. If, however, the easement is not in writing but is oral, a license is created and not an easement. However, an easement in favor of the conveyer that is appurtenant to the tract retained is called a reservation.

2. Creation by Implication

An easement by implication is created by operation of law and is an exception to the statute of frauds. In order for there to be a valid easement by implication, four requirements must be met: (1) at the time of the conveyance, one part of the land is being used for the benefit of the other part; (2) the use is apparent; (3) the use is continuous; and (4) the use is either reasonably or strictly necessary to the enjoyment of the dominant tract.

3. Creation by Necessity

An easement by necessity is created if the owner of a tract of land divides the tract into two lots and deprives one lot access to a public road.

4. Creation by Prescription

An easement by prescription is created by an adverse use of the servient estate by the dominant estate. An easement by prescription requires: (1) adverse use; (2) continuous use for the statutory period of time; (3) open and notorious use; and (4) no interruption.

C. Terminating an Easement

1. Estoppel

An easement is terminated by estoppel when the servient estate reasonably relies on the conduct of the owner of the dominant estate and uses his servient estate in a manner inconsistent with the existence of the easement and it would be inequitable to use the easement further.

2. **The Necessity is Over**
   Once the necessity is over, the easement that was created due to the necessity is terminated.

3. **Destruction of the Property**
   If the easement is a structure and it is involuntarily destroyed, the easement is terminated.

4. **Condemnation**
   Condemnation of the servient estate will terminate the easement. However, most jurisdictions allow compensation for any lost value.

5. **Abandonment**
   If the dominant tenant intends to abandon the use of the easement, the easement is terminated. However, non-use of an easement does not terminate an easement. If there is non-use of the easement and an intent to abandon the easement, the easement is terminated.

6. **Merger**
   When both the dominant and serviant estates merge into a single possession by another person, any easements present are terminated.

D. Licenses
A license is a permit for one to come onto the land possessed by another without being considered a trespasser. A license is a privilege and therefore can be revoked at the will of the licensor unless it is coupled with an interest.

CREATION OF EASEMENTS

Willard v. First Church of Christ, Scientist

7 Cal. 3d 473, 102 Cal. Rptr. 739, 498 P.2d 987 (1972)

FACTS

Genevieve McGuigan owned lots 19 and 20 in Pacifica, California. Both lots were located across the street from the First Church of Christ, Scientist, of which she was a member. She allowed vacant lot 20 to be used as a parking lot during church services and sold lot 19 to one Peterson, who used the building on the lot as an office. Thereafter, wanting to resell lot 19, Peterson listed it with Plaintiff-Realtor Donald E. Willard. Willard expressed an interest in both lots and he and Peterson signed a deposit receipt for the sale of the lots and Peterson delivered a deed for both in fee simple. Peterson did not own lot 20 at the time of the sale to Willard, so he approached McGuigan with an offer to buy it. McGuigan would only sell the lot if the church could continue to use it for parking. She then had the church's attorney draw up a provision in the deed to the lot stating that the change of ownership was subject to an easement for automobile parking during church hours and that such easement was to run with the land only so long as the property was used for church purposes. After the easement language was added to the deed, McGuigan sold the property to Peterson and Peterson recorded the deed. Thereafter, Plaintiff paid Peterson the agreed upon purchase price and received his deed about a week later; Willard recorded this deed. However, the Peterson-Willard deed did not mention the easement for the parking lot by the church. It appears that Peterson mentioned the church's intentions with respect to the lot in question, but did not inform Willard of the actual easement clause in (his) McGuigan-Peterson deed. The easement clause became known to him several months after his purchase of the lot and he thereafter initiated an action to quiet title against the church. Testimony was proffered by McGuigan that she bought lot 20 with the specific intention of providing parking for the church and that she would not have sold it knowing that the church could no longer use it for parking. The trial court held that both McGuigan and Peterson proposed to convey the easement to the church but that the clause in the deed was invalid because this interest may not vest in a third party (a stranger to the title).

I Can a grantor (seller) reserve an easement in the property for a third party when such property is conveyed to a grantee (buyer)?

R A grantor can reserve an easement in property granted to a third party other than the grantee.

A A grantor can reserve an easement in property granted to a third party other than the grantee. The old common law rule that stated that one cannot reserve an interest in property to a stranger in title is no longer followed in this jurisdiction. Historically, common law courts opposed a person reserving an interest in property to a stranger to the title. And while California availed itself of this rule, we do not feel restrained by such antiquated feudal concerns today. In modern times, we treat property grants the same way as contracts thus carrying out the main objective of the law: the intent of the grantor. Thus, awards under the old common law model would lead to inequitable consequences because the original grantee had in all likelihood paid a lesser price for the land in return for permitting a particular use of the land to carry on. In the instant case, Plaintiff Willard has not proven that he had relied upon the old common law rule in buying the lot. Nor can he argue that there was a bias against him because the lot was idle and vacant for a prolonged period. To be sure, the lot was in use by the church for parking during the entire time the plaintiff was negotiating to purchase it. Thus, in this case, the interest of the grantors prevail over any interest the grantees may have had had the old rule been followed. Taking the clause in its entirety, it is apparent that both McGuigan and Peterson proposed to convey the easement for parking to the church.

C A grantor can reserve an easement in property granted to a third party other than the grantee. Judgment reversed.

Holbrook v. Taylor

532 S.W.2d 763 (1976)

FACTS

This action was brought about to establish the right to use a roadway over the unenclosed, hilly woodlands of another. In 1942, Defendants-Appellants Mr. and Mrs. Holbrook purchased property. In 1944, they allowed a mining road to be cut on the property which was used for that purpose until 1949. Defendants were paid a royalty for the use of the road during that period and for that purpose. In 1964, Plaintiffs-Appellees Taylor (the "Taylors") bought a three acre building site adjoining defendants' property and built a house on the land the following year. Defendants allowed the plaintiffs and their builders to use the thoroughfare for access to and from the building and for development of the house. After the house was finished, plaintiffs still used the road frequently. Plaintiffs used the road without incident until 1970. At trial, evidence was offered to show plaintiffs were permitted to use and repair the roadway so that they could reach their house, as this was the only point where a road could be created to provide access thereto. At a cost of roughly $100, plaintiffs broadened the road, put in a culvert and paved part of it. Sometime thereafter, defendants wanted the plaintiffs to provide a signed written instrument relieving them (defendants) of any liability in the event someone was hurt on the roadway. Plaintiffs-Appellees contend that this request was a calculated effort on defendants' part to force plaintiffs to buy the land upon which the road was placed for $500. Thereafter, an argument ensued and the defendants raised a steel cable across the road to block ingress and egress to the property and erected "no trespassing" signs. Sometime later, the Taylors filed this action to get rid of any and all obstructions and to declare their right to use the road without interference.

I Can an easement be established by (1) prescription or (2) by estoppel?

R When a person has been granted a license which includes the right to make improvements and does so at considerable expense in reliance on the license, the licensor may not revoke the license and restore his premises to its former condition after the licensee has exercised the privilege given by the license.

A We first address the issue of an easement established by prescription. At all times prior to 1965, the use of the roadway by the appellees was with the permission of the appellants. There is no evidence to suggest that the use of the roadways was, at any time, adverse, continuous or uninterrupted. Thus, the trial court was fully justified in its finding that the right and use of the easement was not established by prescription. We now turn to the issue of whether an easement was established by estoppel. An easement can be established by estoppel when the person making use of the property does so with the permission of the property owner; and courts have long recognized this right with respect to the use of a roadway over another person's land. We follow this rule first recognized in *Lashey Telephone Co. v. Durban* (a licensor may not revoke a license, which includes the right to erect structures and acquire an interest in the land similar to the easement, after the license has been exercised the privilege of a license and erected improvements on the land at considerable expense). In the instant case, it is clearly evident that the plaintiffs made use of the road with the consent and/or the tacit approval of the Holbrooks. Plaintiffs used the road to build and improve their home and then widened and kept up the road at an added cost to them. These facts clearly satisfy the *Lashey* rule prerequisites, and, as such, plaintiffs' license to use the road is irrevocable as their right to such use has been established by estoppel.

C A license cannot be revoked by the licensor after the licensee has made improvement(s) on the land at a considerable expense in reliance on the license. Judgment affirmed.

Shepard v. Purvine

196 Or. 348, 248 P.2d 352 (1952)

FACTS

The facts of this case are apparently as follows: Plaintiff Shepard and Defendant Purvine were neighbors and close friends but were not "dealing at arms length" with respect to the ensuing agreement. Both agreed to a transfer of property rights that was, in effect, a license for a right-of-way. Their agreement was made orally, without a written deed. This was done because, under the circumstances, for plaintiff to have insisted on a deed would have been embarrassing; as it would have been to express doubt in his friend's integrity. One's word was considered as good as his bond. Thus no formal transfer of rights were established. Thereafter, presumably, a disagreement over the license occurred and plaintiff filed this suit.

I Is an oral license valid?

R An oral license may bind as effectively as one written.

A To these parties, one's word was as good as one's bond. If Plaintiff Shepard firmly required a written deed to spell out the details of their agreement, it would have been construed by his friend (Defendant Purvine) as a manifestation of mistrust in his (Purvine's) honesty and integrity. Nevertheless, plaintiff cannot be found negligent by failing to obtain a formal transfer of the contracted rights because an oral license, carried out with due haste, is just as binding, valid and irrevocable as an easement conveyed by deed.

C An oral license may bind as effectively as one written.

Henry v. Dalton

98 R.I. 150, 151 A.2d 362 (1959)

FACTS

Facts omitted.

I Can a licensor (property owner) who gave a licensee an oral license to do an act on his property arbitrarily revoke the license, even if the licensee has expended money in reliance thereupon?

R An oral license to do an act on the land of the licensor is revocable at the option of the licensor, even if the licensee has spent money in reliance upon the license.

A In this case, we follow the rule first established in *Crossdale v. Lanigan* (Lanigan had given Mr. Crossdale an oral license to remove a wall built on Mr. Lanigan's property) whereby an oral license is a valid license to do an act on the land of the licensor, but is nonetheless revocable at the licensor's will. This rule is still applicable when the licensor intended to grant a lasting right to the licensee or where the licensee expended money in reliance upon the license. The rule is supported by both statute and by public policy and precludes the encumbrance of lands by oral limitations which can certainly be misinterpreted and misapplied. In addition, we note that the law differentiating licenses from irrevocable contracts is not so well-defined. Thus, it is our opinion that it is better to set forth an unambiguous rule, rather than having a court balance the equities of each case where such a license and its revocation is at issue. While the statute of frauds may be applicable to some extent, there is no proof that the instant license is tainted by fraud in any way. Since the instrument here is basically an easement, we hold it ought to be dependent upon the grant stated in a written instrument.

C An oral license to do an act on the land of the licensor is revocable at the option of the licensor, even if the licensee has spent money in reliance upon the license.

Van Sandt v. Royster

148 Kan. 495, 83 P.2d 698 (1938)

FACTS

In 1904, Laura Bailey owned a plot of land in Chanute, Kansas. Her plot was divided into three lots numbered, from west to east, as lots 4, 20 and 19. Bailey's home was located on lot 4, on the most eastern part of her land. Earlier that year, the City of Chanute built a public sewer on Highland Avenue, which ran parallel to lot 19. Highland Avenue ran alongside of lot 19. Shortly after, a lateral drain was build, spanning all of the lots and running from the Bailey home on lot 4, across lots 20 and 19 into the public sewer. Also in 1904, Bailey sold lot 19 to John Jones and sold lot 20 to Murphy. Both lots were conveyed by general warranty deed. Each person then constructed a house on his own lot. Title to lot 20 was later conveyed to Defendant Louise Royster and Co-Defendant Gray took title to lot 4 when lots 19 and 20 were sold. By 1924, lot 19 had been conveyed to Plaintiff Van Zandt, who continued to own and live there. In March 1936, Van Zandt discovered his basement had been flooded with raw sewage. He discovered the cause was a break in the sewer drain which extended across the properties of Royster (lot 4) and Gray (lot 20). This drain pipe was located several feet underground and was not visible without an excavation. In fact, there was nothing on the ground behind the houses to indicate the existence of a drain or its link to the houses. Van Zandt sued to enjoin Royster and Gray from making use of the drain, but the trial court held for the defendants. Thereafter, Van Zandt appealed and argued that a sub-surface easement was not created and that even if one was, it cannot be a valid easement as he was not given any notice of it. Defendants counter-argued that an easement was created by implied reservation on the severance of the servient estate from the dominant estate of the deed when lot 19 was sold to Jones by Bailey. Defendants further argue that there is a valid easement by prescription.

I Is an easement by implication (one of strict necessity) created when the easement was in use by an earlier title-holder but was not readily detectable by the party to whom the property was conveyed?

R The creation of an easement by implication depends upon the conditions under which the conveyance was made, including the extent to which the prior use was or might have been known by the parties; thus, each party is presumed to have notice of all reasonably necessary uses which are apparent upon a reasonably prudent investigation.

A The creation of an easement by implication depends upon the conditions under which the conveyance was made, including the extent to which the prior use was or might have been known by the parties. Thus each party is assumed to have notice of all reasonably necessary uses which are apparent upon a reasonably prudent investigation. An easement is an interest in land which one person has in another's. Typically, an owner cannot have an easement in his own land but is permitted to use one part of his land to the benefit of another part of the land; often called a quasi-easement. The part of the land that benefits from this use is a quasi-dominant tenement, while the part of the land burdened with the particular use is a quasi-servant tenement. An implied easement arises when one party interferes with the intentions of another party; where such interference is drawn from the circumstances, not the language of the conveyance. These circumstances take account of the extent to which prior use was known or might have been known by the respective parties. Thus, all parties are presumed to have notice of all reasonably necessary uses which would be apparent upon a reasonably prudent inspection. In the instant case, when Jones bought lot 19, he was aware of the lateral sewer drain across all three lots and knew it was originally build for Bailey's use. The easement for the sewer was necessary for the use and enjoyment of Bailey's property. Of critical importance here is that an easement can be implied on the basis of necessity alone such that Van Zandt cannot claim a lack of notice with respect to the lateral sewer when he bought his property. Both plaintiff and his wife made a careful inspection of the property; they knew the house had modern plumbing and they knew that the plumbing had to drain into a sewer.

C The creation of an easement by implication depends upon the conditions under which the conveyance was made, including the extent to which the prior use was or might have been known by the parties; thus, each party is presumed to have notice of all reasonably necessary uses which are apparent upon a reasonably prudent investigation. Judgment affirmed.

Othen v. Rosier

148 Tex. 485, 226 S.W.2d 622

FACTS

The entire 2493 acres of the Tone Survey was once owned by one Hill. By mesne (intermediate) conveyances, Hill's 100 acre track eventually came into the possession of Defendant Estella Rozier and others in 1924. In 1897, Hill conveyed a 60 acre tract by mesne conveyances to Plaintiff Albert Othen in 1904. It was southeast of, and contiguous to, the 100 acre tract of the Roziers leaving Hill ownership of a 53 acre tract just east of the 100 acre tract and a 16.31 acre tract just west of the 60 acre tract. Hill conveyed these two tracts to separate buyers on January 26, 1899. These buyers afterward conveyed the 53 acre tract to Othen in 1913 and the 16.31 acre track to Rozier in 1924, respectively. Thus, Othen's entire property consisting of both conveyances was not contiguous with any of the highways that border the Tone Survey to the north and south. Prior to this action, plaintiff would reach the main roadway, Belt Line Road, by walking through a gate on the western line of his 60 acre tract, then along the eastern line of the defendant's 16.31 acre tract, and then along a fenced lane which runs along the south side of defendant's 100 acres. This lane led to a gate which opened out onto Belt Line Road. Within close proximity of the gate was the defendant's home, orchard and barn. The lane was used by the defendants to haul wood and to allow their livestock access to the 16.31 acre tract for grazing. All repairs and maintenance to the lane were carried out solely by the defendants themselves. At some point, pooling rain water endangered the use of the road and threatened to erode the defendant's farmland, so they built a long levee the along the southern boundary of the road. For weeks at a time, this levee muddied the land making it impassable except by horseback. Plaintiff brought an action seeking (1) a temporary injunction to restrain the defendants from using the levee and (2) a mandatory injunction to prevent the defendants from interfering with plaintiff's use of the lane. The trial court held that plaintiff had an easement of necessity along the lane and ordered the defendants to guarantee that it remain open and operational. The Court of Civil Appeals affirmed the judgment, but later reversed the injunction holding that it was imprecise. On rehearing, the Appellate Court concluded that Plaintiff Othen held neither an easement of necessity nor an easement by prescription.

I Can an easement be implied when the party seeking the easement has not proven its use as a necessity or that its use was allowed with the permission of the neighboring property owner?

R An easement by implied reservation can only be created when it is shown that there (1) was unity of ownership between the alleged dominant and servient estates; (2) that the easement is a necessity and not a mere convenience; and (3) that the necessity existed at the time of the severance of the two estates. An easement by prescription can only be acquired if the use of the easement was adverse.

A An easement by implied reservation can only be created when it is shown that there (1) was unity of ownership between the alleged dominant and servient estates; (2) that the easement is a necessity and not a mere convenience; and (3) that the necessity existed at the time of the severance of the two estates. We note, however, that an easement by prescription can only be acquired if the use of the easement was adverse. The entire Tone Survey was, at one time, owned by Hill. Thus the "unity of ownership" element of the rule is satisfied. In spite of this, there is no proof to suggest that the roadway was a necessity when Hill conveyed the 100 track. It seems as though the roadway was just a convenience as Hill could have just as easily crossed the 53 acre tract and gone around the 100 acre tract to get to Belt Line Road. At this time, however, no easement existed over the 16.31 acre tract because Hill still owned that land in 1896, and an easement can not be created where both tracts of land are owned by the same title holder. The fact that plaintiff's land is completely land-locked by his neighbor's property does not necessarily mandate a right-of-way of necessity for the plaintiff over the neighbor's estate. Thus, the plaintiff is precluded from recovering under an easement by necessity theory and an easement by prescription can only be maintained if the use of the easement here was adverse. It was not. In the instant case, the lane had been fenced both to the north and south since 1906. Both the defendants and their tenants have used it for general farm purposes as well as to move livestock to pasture with defendants' permission or at least its tacit approval. Thus, Othen's use of the path could not have developed into a prescriptive right. We likewise reject plaintiff's proof of his use of the roadway prior to 1906, deeming it too vague to establish a prescriptive right.

C An easement by implied reservation can only be created when it is shown that there (1) was unity of ownership between the alleged dominant and servient estates; (2) that the easement is a necessity and not a mere convenience; and (3) that the necessity existed at the time of the severance of the two estates. Judgment affirmed.

Mathews v. Bay Head Improvement Association

95 N.J. 306, 47 A.2d 355 (1984)

FACTS

The Borough of Bay Head is a narrow strip of land about 1 ¼ miles long bordered by the Borough of Point Pleasant Beach on the north and the Borough of Mantoloking to the south.. A beach runs along the entire length of Bay Head adjacent to the Atlantic Ocean. The beach is surrounded by 76 separate parcels of land; 70 are owned by private individuals and six are owned by Defendant Bay Head Improvement Association (Association); founded in 1910 but became a nonprofit corporation in 1932. The Association exists to promote the best interests of the county. Nine streets run perpendicular to the beach and end at the dry sand. The Association owns the land at the end of seven of these streets extending through the upper dry sand to the mean high water line also called the foreshore, or wet sand area. In addition, the Association owns six shore front properties. Three of these properties adjoin one another and combine to create 310 ft. of frontage facing the ocean. The Association controls and supervises its beach property during the summer, employing some 40 personnel as lifeguards, beach cleaners and policemen. The beach entrances are patrolled to make certain that only those Association members (Bay Head residents) and their guests can enter, thereby enforcing membership rules. During the summer, between the hours of 10 a.m. and 5:30 p.m., only Association members and local fishermen are allowed to use the Association beach and the public is permitted use of the upper dry sand area from 5:30 p.m. to 10 a.m. only. Public access to the foreshore is allowed through the Borough of Point Pleasant Beach on the north or from the Borough of Mantoloking on the south. The public advocate for the Borough of Point Pleasant via Mathews maintained that the defendant denied the general public (1) access to public trust lands along the beach in Bay Head and (2) use of the private property along the ocean under the public trust doctrine.

I Does the public have a right to use and enjoy the tidal lands ancillary to its right to access and use privately owned lands not owned by the municipality?

R Under the public trust doctrine, the public's right to use the tidal lands includes the right to gain access through and to use the privately owned dry sand areas not owned by the municipality via a quasi-public body as is reasonably necessary.

A Under the public trust doctrine, the public's right to use the tidal lands includes the right to gain access through and to use the privately owned dry sand areas not owned by the municipality via a quasi-public body as is reasonably necessary. Under the public trust doctrine, the ownership, dominion and sovereignty over the land covered by title waters is for the common use of all people. This land typically extends from the ocean to the mean high water level and the public's right to use this land and surrounding water historically included maritime and fishing rights. Extension of the public trust doctrine in *Borough of Neptune City v. Borough of Avon-by-the-sea* to include bathing, swimming and other shore activities is consonant with and furthers the general welfare. This right must be respected. Implementation of this right, nonetheless, may implicate the right to traverse land traditionally restricted to the public. But without some type of access, the public's right to use the wet sand area would be futile. We note that the right to traverse private land is not without its limits. But so long as <u>reasonable</u> access is provided, the public interest is satisfied and the public trust doctrine is satisfied. In this case, the activities of the Association are not unlike those of a town or borough. Thus, the quasi-public nature of the Association is readily apparent and, as a result, membership must be allowed to the public. We thus hold that the general public will now be able to use the beaches during the summer months throughout the day.

C Under the public trust doctrine, the public's right to use the tidal lands includes the right to gain access through and to use the privately owned dry sand areas not owned by the municipality via a quasi-public body as is reasonably necessary. Judgment entered against the Association.

ASSIGNABILITY OF EASEMENTS

Miller v. Lutheran Conference & Camp Association

331 Pa. 241, 200 A. 646, 130 A.L.R. 1245 (1938)

FACTS

In September 1895, Frank Miller, brother Rufus Miller and others created the Pocono Spring Water Ice Co. (Company) to create Lake Naomi via a 14 ft. dam which they proposed to build across the Tunkhannock Creek. This company was created for the purpose of "erecting a dam for pleasure boating, commerce, skating, fishing, and the cutting, storing and selling of ice." By a deed dated March 28, 1899, the Company granted to Plaintiff Frank Miller and "his heirs and assigns forever, the exclusive right to fish and boat in all the waters of the Company." On December 17, 1900, Frank Miller granted to Rufus Miller and his heirs and assigns forever a ¼ interest which had been conferred to him in the 1899 deed. That afternoon, plaintiff and Rufus formed a partnership to rent boats and houses on the lake. Plaintiff assumed a ¾ interest in the partnership and Rufus was allocated a ¼ interest. Rufus died on October 11, 1925. Four years later, the administrators of Rufus Miller's estate granted a one year license to Defendant Lutheran Conference & Camp Association (Association) essentially allowing the defendant's members to use the lake for boating, bathing and fishing with a percentage of the revenue generated by such activity to be paid to the Rufus's estate. This precipitated plaintiff's filing of an action in equity alleging that the Association was really planning to license its own guests to use the lake. Plaintiff requested an injunction to prevent future trespassing by the Association. The trial court granted the injunction. Plaintiff claimed that no boating rights were ever conveyed to him by the Company through the 1899 grant, thus he neither had nor could have transferred any such rights to Rufus. What's more, plaintiff argues, even if such bathing rights were vested in him, such privileges were easements in gross and as such were neither alienable nor divisible. The Defendant (Association) responded alleging that the 1899 deed conveyed the bathing privileges to the plaintiff in addition to the boating and fishing rights or, in the alternative, that both Plaintiff Frank Miller and Rufus Miller acquired the bathing privileges by prescription, thus rendering them alienable and divisible.

I Does one of two owners of an easement in gross have the right to further assign those same rights to a third party?

R When an easement in gross is owned by at least two persons, any actions involving the easement must be made with the consent of all the owners; the easement must be treated as "one stock," meaning it cannot be conveyed as a shared common right by only one party.

A When an easement in gross is owned by at least two persons, any actions involving the easement must be made with the consent of all the owners; it must be treated as "one stock," meaning it cannot be conveyed as a shared common right by only one party. In the instant case, the 1899 deed cannot be interpreted as transferring bathing rights to Frank Miller as the deed plainly affirms a grant of limited rights to fish and boat without any mention of a right to bath. We acknowledge, though, that Frank Miller may have obtained bathing rights by prescription. The law does allow prohibit the pleasure of an easement in gross whose title may be acquired by prescription. Over time, Lake Naomi has expanded to become a fashionable summer resort, with its bathing and boating services having some special significance. Accordingly, it would be exceedingly unfair to hold that the Miller Brothers did not hold title to the bathing rights by prescription which were just as important as the boating and fishing privileges actually conveyed to them by the 1899 deed. While the assignability of easements in gross, such as the fishing, boating, and bathing rights involved here, has been debated by some authorities, we focus here on only their divisibility. These easements must be used or exercise as a whole. In other words, a single owner cannot convey a shared common right without the consent of the other owner(s). In this case, it looks as if Plaintiff Frank Miller did not want to grant his brother, Rufus, the additional authority to be able to re-divide and carve out the various lake rights. Indeed, it is apparent that plaintiff intended for he and his brother to use their rights collectively for the businesses, as evidenced by the unequal allocation of the profits between the two, proportional to their respective partnership interests. Taken as a whole, the evidence indicates that these easements should be considered "one stock" whereby any actions with respect to the easements must be made with the shared consent of all the owners and not regarded as a common right to be exercised by only one party acting unilaterally.

C When an easement in gross is owned by at least two persons, any actions involving the easement must be made with the consent of all the owners; the easement must be treated as "one stock," meaning it cannot be conveyed as a shared common right by only one party.

SCOPE OF EASEMENTS

Brown v. Voss

105 Wash. 2d 366, 715 P.2d 514 (1986)

FACTS

In 1952, the predecessors in title of parcel A granted a private road easement (the "initial grant") across the property to the then owners of parcel B for "ingress to and egress from" parcel B. In 1973, the Vosses (defendants) acquired parcel A and on April 1, 1977, the Browns (plaintiffs) bought parcel B and thereafter parcel C from another party on July 31, 1977. The prior title holders of lot C were not participants in the easement conveyance. Plaintiffs Brown intended to construct a home that would span the B-C property lines. The Browns began developing both lots in late 1977, but by early 1979 Defendants Voss took steps to halt the Browns from using the easement. To that end, defendants placed logs, a concrete pit and a chain-link fence to block access to the road. Up to this point, the plaintiffs had expended over $11,000 to clear the properties and develop the land. Plaintiffs filed suit to get rid of the obstacles on the roadway and asked the court for damages and an injunction against further interference with their use of the road. The defendants countersued for damages and also requested an injunction against the plaintiffs to prevent them from further using the road. As to the respective parties' claims for damages, the trial court awarded nominal damages of $1 to both parties. With respect to both injunction requests, the court reasoned that if the defendant's injunction were granted, parcel C would be landlocked and the plaintiffs would not be able to make use of their property. Moreover, enforcement of such an injunction would not be feasible. Conversely, should the defendants' injunction be denied, the trial court reasoned, the defendants would not suffer any substantial injury. Thus, the plaintiffs' injunction request was granted and the defendants' injunction was denied and the plaintiffs were allowed to continue using the easement as long as the parcels were used solely for a single-family residence.

I Can a holder of an easement traverse the servient estate to reach both the original dominant estate and a subsequently acquired parcel when there will be no increased burden on the servient estate?

R If an easement is appurtenant (belonging) to a particular parcel of land, and benefits its owner in the use of that particular parcel of land, any extension of the easement to other parcels of land constitutes a misuse of the easement.

A The terms of the grant and the intentions of the parties help define the scope of the right acquired through the easement and, in this case, derive directly from the express grant made in 1952. The initial grant allowed the predecessors in title of parcel B to obtain a private easement across parcel A and the right to use it for ingress and egress to parcel B. Thus plaintiffs surely obtained these same rights with respect to parcel B, but could not obtain these same easement rights with regard to parcel C because parcel C was not part of the original dominant tenement under the language of the initial grant. An easement which confers a benefit to an owner in his use of a tract of land is limited to that parcel only, such that any extension of the use of the easement to other tracts of land constitutes a misuse of the easement. Thus, while plaintiffs argue that their use of the easement to gain access to a single-family home located partially on parcel B and partially on parcel C amounts to a minor technical misuse of the easement, we conclude that it is nonetheless a misuse. However, this conclusion does not mean that the Vosses (defendants) are thus entitled to injunctive relief. The relief afforded by an injunction is an equitable one, and, as such, we give deference to the findings of the trial court unless an abuse of discretion has been established. No such abuse is evident in this case.

C If an easement is appurtenant (belonging) to a particular parcel of land, and benefits its owner in the use of that particular parcel of land, any extension of the easement to other parcels of land constitutes a misuse of the easement. Judgment of the Court of Appeals is reversed and judgment of the trial court is affirmed.

TERMINATION OF EASEMENTS

Preseault v. United States
100 F.3d 1525 (Fed. Cir. 1996)

FACTS

The Preseaults (plaintiffs) owned a fee simple interest in a tract of land along the shore of Lake Champlain in Burlington, Vermont on which they had a home. A right-of-way ran across several previously separate properties composing the track. In 1899, the right-of-way was acquired by the Rutland-Canadian Railroad Co. which operated a railroad on the strip after constructing tracks across the land. By 1975, the railroad tracks were dismantled and carted away from that section of the right-of-way on the plaintiffs' land. Eight years later, Congress enacted the Rails-to-Trails Act which effectively (1) preserved defunct railroad lines for future rail use and (2) allowed the public recreational use of the right-of-way. Specifically, the Act authorized the Interstate Commerce Commission (ICC) to sanction abandonment of the rail line or to permit discontinuance of rail service and convey the right-of-way to any public/private entities willing to preserve the rail corridor as a public trail. By 1986, the ICC endorsed an agreement between the Virginia Railway, the State of Vermont and the City of Burlington to cease rail service over the plaintiffs' land and to continue using the once active railroad line as a public trail. Plaintiffs first brought an action against the ICC arguing the unconstitutionality of Rails-to-Trails Act but the U.S. Supreme Court held the Act constitutional. Plaintiffs next brought an action against the United States government arguing that the Government (defendant), by way of the ICC, effected a taking of the plaintiffs' property when it sanctioned the conversion of the rail line to public trail use relying on the holding in *Loretto v. Teleprompter Manhattan CATV Corp.* The trial court disagreed and ruled in favor of the Government. Plaintiffs appealed.

I (1) Does government's use of the right-of-way go beyond the scope of the easement thus constituting a "taking" of the servient estate? (2) Was the easement terminated by non use?

R Only where the non use is coupled with a definitive act demonstrating either a present intent to surrender the easement or a use incompatible with its future continuance can an easement be terminated by abandonment.

A (1) Yes. When the Government's use of a track of land goes beyond the scope of the easement a "taking" of the servient tenement is effected. Here, we are in agreement with the trial court that the right-of-way was at some point an easement. Even if the easement still existed in 1986, we find that the Government's use of the land for a recreational trail is not within the scope of the easement. Although a public recreational trail may be described as a "roadway" for the transportation of persons, its "public" nature and usage is clearly different from the "commercial enterprise," character and use of the transportation of goods and persons via railroad. And while the scope of an easement may be modified over time, this may only occur if the change is consistent with the terms of the original grant. This did not happen here. Thus, we hold that the change in use of the railroad corridor to a recreational trail is not consistent with the terms of the original railroad easement. (2) No. Vermont law recognizes and follows the well-established rule of law that an easement may not terminated by mere non use. Thus, in order to validly terminate an easement by abandonment, there must be a voluntary relinquishment or surrender of the property, or an interest in property, coupled with an affirmative act by the owner of the dominant tenement which irrefutably and explicitly displays a present intent to surrender the easement without any intention of resuming enjoyment or possession, or of vesting it in anyone else. Here, we agree with the trial judge that the removal of the rails and all related equipment resulted in an abandonment. It is irrelevant that the means to restore the railway service over the rail corridor still exists. To be sure, we note that one irrefutable piece of evidence in favor of abandonment is that fact that following the closure of the railroad line and the removal of the railroad tracts in the early to mid 1970's, neither the State nor the railroad had made any attempt to reinstate railroad service on the line. Lastly, we note that where there is physical entry upon the private lands of another by the Government or one of its agents, a taking has occurred. It is irrelevant that the Government may put into play a series of events which result in the taking of private property through a state or local actor, the consequences still mandate a finding that a taking has occurred and that the Government must provide adequate compensation to those whose property interests were affected. In this case, the Government decided to impinge upon the Voss's property interests, thus the Fifth Amendment compels compensation.

C Only where the non use is coupled with a definitive act demonstrating either a present intent to surrender the easement or a use incompatible with its future continuance can an easement be terminated by abandonment. Reversed and remanded.

VII. COVENANTS AT LAW AND EQUITABLE SERVITUDES

Covenants at law serve to bind future owners of land who are not parties to the original contract by enforcing promises against successors in interest of the original parties. At law, such promises are enforced as covenants at law and in equity as equitable servitudes. Covenants at law could be either affirmative or negative. Affirmative covenants are promises to do something, whereas negative covenants are promises not to do something.

A. Common Elements Between Covenants at Law and Equitable Servitudes

1. Touch and Concern the Land

Both covenants at law and equitable servitudes must touch and concern the land. This means that both the benefits and burdens placed on the land must pass to succeeding landholders.

2. Intent to Run With the Land

Both covenants at law and equitable servitudes must be intended by the covenantor and covenantee to "run with the land." This is accomplished by language which clearly states the intent of the promise to "run with the land."

3. Writing

In order for there to be a valid covenant at law or equitable servitude, there must be a writing to satisfy the statute of frauds. However, in the case of **negative equitable servitudes,** where a developer divides land and some deeds contain negative covenants and some do not, the negative covenants will be binding on all parcels of land even without a writing if there is a common scheme of development and the owner had notice.

B. Additional Elements for Covenants at Law

1. Privity

a. Vertical Privity
Vertical privity is a relationship between successors in interest involving covenanting parties. For example, if A transfers to B, and B transfers to C, A and C are in vertical privity.

b. Horizontal Privity
Horizontal privity is a relationship involving a common grantor. For example, if A sells a plot of land to B, and B sells the plot to C; then A, B and C are in horizontal privity.

2. Damages

The remedy for a breach of a covenant at law is damages.

C. Additional Elements for Equitable Servitudes

1. Notice

Notice could be actual, constructive or inquiry and must be in writing.

2. Damages

The remedy for a breach of an equitable servitude is an injunction.

COVENANTS ENFORCEABLE IN EQUITY: EQUITABLE SERVITUDES

Tulk v. Moxhay

4(1848) 2 Phillips 774, 41 Eng. Rep. 1143

FACTS

Plaintiff Tulk was the owner of several houses and a vacant parcel in Leicester Square. The Square was enclosed by an iron railing and stone work. That same year, Tulk sold the vacant lot in Leicester Square to one Elms. The deed contained a covenant which stated that Elms and his heirs and assigns would maintain the property as a square garden and as public pleasure ground, in an open state and "uncovered with buildings." This property passed by various mesne conveyances (a conveyance which is between the first grantee and the present holder in the chain of title) from Elms eventually to Defendant Moxhay. However, Defendant's deed contained no similar covenant against the construction of buildings on the Square, but defendant admitted that he purchased the land with notice of the original covenant in the 1808 deed. Defendant Moxhay tried to alter the character of the square garden and asserted the right to build on the garden as he saw fit, but plaintiff filed an injunction to prevent Moxhay from using the pleasure ground and garden for any purpose other than its original open state, devoid of any structures built thereupon.

I Can a covenant be enforced against a purchaser of land when that purchaser acquired the land through mesne conveyances with knowledge of the prior covenant?

R Where a person purchases land with notice of a covenant, that covenant will be enforced in equity against him.

A An unambiguous covenant existed between Plaintiff Tulk and Elms, restricting Elms's use of the land he purchased. It is clear that by the terms of the conveyance, Elms promised to use his land adjoining the Square and neighboring plaintiff's remaining houses and land as a square garden only. Thus, if Defendant Moxhay were permitted to purchase this same land from Elms and violate the covenant, then any title holder who to tried to sell his land surrounding the Square, like Plaintiff Tulk, would run the risk having it rendered worthless because its sale price would be adversely affected by the breached covenant. Defendant likely paid less for the land so burdened by the covenant. So to allow the defendant to build on the land would be to effectively allow him to receive unburdened land for the reduced price land burdened by a covenant. This is clearly inequitable and can not be allowed. To do so would permit the defendant to resell the unburdened of land and a higher place, and thus be unjustly enriched. Therefore, we hold that if a covenant is attached to property by its original owner, no one with notice of that covenant can purchase the property and not be bound by the covenant.

C Where a person purchases land with notice of a covenant, that covenant will be enforced in equity against him. Decision affirmed.

CREATION OF COVENANTS

Sanborn v. Mclean

(1925) 233 Mich. 227, 206 N.W. 496, 60 A.L.R. 1212

FACTS

On December 28, 1892, Robert J. and Joseph R. McLaughlin, then owners of lots on Collingwood Avenue in Detroit, deeded lots 37 to 41 and 50 to 62, inclusive, with restrictions that provided "no residence shall be erected on said premises, which shall cost less than $2,500, and nothing but residences shall be erected upon said premises. Said premises shall from on Helene (now Collingwood) avenue and be placed no nearer than 20 feet from the front street line." On July 24, 1893, both individuals collectively conveyed lots 17 to 21, 78 to 82 and 98 with the same restrictions. On September 7, 1893, the McLaughlins sold lot 86, which, by mesne conveyances, was eventually conveyed to the Mcleans (defendants) by a deed which did not contain these restrictions. The defendants thereafter occupied a partially built house on the lot whose construction was eventually completed by Mr. Mclean. Sometime later, the defendants commenced construction of a gasoline filling station at the rear of their lot. Plaintiff-neighbor Sanborn, who owned the adjacent lot, filed for an injunction. Defendants were enjoined by decree and an appeal followed.

I When a lot is purchased in a subdivision and does not contain a restriction(s) in the deed, but such restrictions are contained in the deeds of adjoining lots in the subdivision from which it was sold, can those restriction(s) be implied in the newly acquired property?

R Where a common plan or scheme exists for the development of a residential subdivision and the buyer takes the property with actual or constructive notice of it, an equitable servitude may be implied even where no written instrument is present.

A Where a developer has set up a common plan or scheme for the creation of a residential subdivision, and a purchaser takes a lot with actual or constructive notice of it, an equitable servitude can be implied on a lot, even where no written instrument is present. In the instant case, the McLaughlins imposed the restrictions on the neighboring lots for their own benefit; specifically for the benefit of the lands they still owned and mainly to carry out the scheme of a residential district. Because the McLaughlins sold these lots with restrictions in order to benefit themselves, the servitude was both mutual and reciprocal; binding buyer and seller (the McLaughlins) alike. Thus, this restriction is deemed a "negative reciprocal easement," and it attached to lot 86 before defendants even acquired the land. Moreover, the restriction was still enforceable against the new owners after they purchased the lot if the defendants acquired it with actual or constructive notice. Because the abstract of title to a lot 86 showed that it was part of a much larger subdivision and because the deeds were on record, the defendants had constructive notice to follow the easement and were thus bound by it. Moreover, the common plan and scheme for the residential neighborhood had been in force for over 30 years and observed by all lot purchasers during that time. We would be hard pressed to believe that defendants did not notice the strictly uniform residential use of the neighboring lots and did not even bother to enquire why all the lots conformed to each other. It is more probable that the defendants had had inquiry notice of the restrictions and were thus bound by them. We note that even the slightest inquiry into the character of the neighborhood would have revealed the easement on a lot 86. Decree affirmed with costs to plaintiffs.

C Where a common plan or scheme exists for the development of a residential subdivision and the buyer takes the property with actual or constructive notice of it, an equitable servitude may be implied even where no written instrument is present.

Neponsit Property Owners' Association, Inc. v. Emigrant Industrial Savings Bank

(1938) 278 N.Y.248, 15 N.E.2d 793

FACTS

In January 1911, the Neponsit Realty Co. filed a land map with the County Clerk's office of a track of land in Queens County that it owned. Neponsit Realty sold lots in the track to purchasers which were developed for strictly residential purposes. In 1917, Neponsit Realty deeded a lot to Mr. and Mrs. Dyer which contained a covenant which stated that the property would be "subject to an annual charge not exceeding in any year, the sum of four dollars;" that the charge was to be used for the "maintenance of the roads, paths, parks, beach, sewers and such other public purposes" and that the fees were payable to Plaintiff-Appellee Neponsit Realty Owners' Association (Association). It was the Association that managed the use of the fees collected. Moreover, the covenant stated that the charges were due on the first of May every year and that failure to pay according to these terms would result in a lien on the owner's land until the fee was paid in full. Defendant-Appellant Emigrant Industrial Savings Bank thereafter acquired title to the Dyer's land at a foreclosure sale. Every deed in the chain of title since the original conveyance by Neponsit Realty subjected the property to the original covenant and defendants' deed was no exception. The plaintiffs sued to foreclose on the lien and enforce the covenant for the annual maintenance fee. Defendants' motion for judgment on the pleadings was denied, so defendant appealed.

I Is an affirmative covenant to pay annual maintenance fees enforceable against successive purchasers of land?

R An affirmative covenant to pay money for improvements or maintenance done in connection with, but not actually on, an area of land "touches and concerns the land" and is thus enforceable against subsequent purchasers.

A We note that the crucial question before us is to what extent the covenant significantly affects the legal rights of the parties bound by it. It is a matter of degree or extent which differentiates a covenant that "runs with the land" from one which does not. A covenant which does not run with the land is simply an agreement between two parties. In this case, an owner in the subdivision obtained a common right of enjoyment, with other property owners, in the roads, beaches, public spaces of the community when he paid the annual fee. However, to allow these areas to be fully enjoyed by all over time, the owners must help pay for their upkeep. As a result, the burden was inseparably attached the land, held by various owners, who collectively enjoy the benefit. Thus, the covenant unequivocally touches and concerns the land. We now turn to the issue of the potential lack of privity of estate between plaintiff and defendant; specifically the argument that plaintiff never owned the public sites referenced in the covenant and that the covenant was created only as the assignee of the property owners. We note that it would be nearly impossible to separate the interests of the two parties; the Association and the individual owners and further note that there is, in essence, privity of estate between the Association and the defendant. An affirmative covenant to pay money for improvements or maintenance done in connection with, but not actually on, an area of land "touches and concerns the land" and is thus enforceable against subsequent purchasers, such that a homeowners' association, as the agent of the property owners, can rightfully enforced the covenant. The order denying a motion by the defendant for judgment on the pleadings is affirmed.

C An affirmative covenant to pay money for improvements or maintenance done in connection with, but not actually on, an area of land "touches and concerns the land" and is thus enforceable against subsequent purchasers.

Caullett v. Stanley Stilwell and Sons, Inc.

(1961) 67 N.J. Super. 111, 170 A.2d 52

FACTS

On January 13, 1959, Defendant-Developer Stanley Stillwell and Sons, Inc. conveyed a one acre lot in Homdel, N.J. to the Cauletts (plaintiff-appellee) by warranty deed in consideration of $4000. This suit was initiated after negotiations collapsed between the parties over a covenant in which the defendant-grantor would have reserved "the right to build or construct an original dwelling or building on said premises." The item is designated in the deed as "running with the land… binding the purchasers, their heirs, executors, administrators and assigns." Plaintiff filed for summary judgment arguing that a contract did not exist between the parties for the construction of any building on said lot. Defendant countered by arguing that one of the material conditions of the sale was that the defendant was to serve as plaintiff's contractor for the construction of a building following the conveyance of the lot in question. Summary judgment was granted by the trial court in favor of the Cauletts (plaintiff) effectively holding that the covenant was not enforceable. Defendant appealed.

I Does a covenant constitute an enforceable covenant restricting the use of plaintiff's land enforceable at law or in equity where it benefits only one of the parties?

R A restrictive covenant does not run with the land either at law or in equity when the benefit it creates does not touch and concern the land.

A A covenant will not run at law or in equity if the benefit it creates is personal (in gross) in nature because such a benefit does not touch and concern the land. The agreement would be a simple personal covenant, but not a real covenant that runs with the land. In order for a covenant to touch and concern the land, and hence be considered a real covenant, it must directly influence the occupation, use, or enjoyment of the land. That is, it must be a promise "respecting the use of the land;" a use which is "not merely casual and which is not merely an incident in the performance of the promise." In this case, the promise between the two parties is, at most, a personal agreement between them, calculated to guarantee revenue for Stillwell after selling the land at fairly low price. Hence, the agreement has no effect on the title. It makes no difference that the deed described a covenant as one running with the land; it is still personal in nature and hence ineffective to that end. Even if the covenant was seen as directly restricting the plaintiff's use of the land, it would still not be enforceable because a commercial advantage would be conferred on only the defendant and not affect any use or value of the land. Moreover, public policy is strongly opposed to impeding the free alienability of property when the act would not enhance the surrounding land and it cannot be enforced as an equitable servitude because that right is mainly dependent on the covenant having been made for the benefit of the land retained by the grantor.

C A restrictive covenant does not run with the land at law or in equity when the benefit it creates would not touch and concern the land. Affirmed.

SCOPE OF COVENANTS

Hill v. Community of Damien of Molokai

121 N.M. 353 (N.M. 1996)

FACTS

Defendant Community of Damon of Molokai (Community), a nonprofit corporation, opened a group home for four individuals with AIDS in the Four Hills planned residential subdivision in Albuquerque, New Mexico. The group home housed four persons who were unrelated to one another and required varying levels of home nursing care. Plaintiffs-Appellees William Hill 3rd and his neighbors were residents who lived on the same dead-end street where the group home was located. After the group home was opened, Hill and the others become aware of an increase in traffic on their street. Thereafter, the neighbors claimed that the use of the property as a group home violated a local, community-wide restrictive covenant which mandated that lots in the area be used only for single-family residences. Plaintiffs filed this action to stop the continued use of the property as a group home arguing that the term "single-family residence" in the restrictive covenant was defined to mean only those persons related by blood or by law and did not include group homes in which unrelated people lived together. The Community responded alleging that the restrictive covenant violated the Federal Fair Housing Act, 42 U.S.C. §§3601-3631 (1988) (FHA), but the trial court nevertheless granted the plaintiffs' injunction request. Defendant Community appealed arguing that the group home is a permanent use under the covenant and, alternatively, that enforcing the covenant would violate the FHA.

I (1) Should the Four Hills restrictive covenant be applied to the Community's Group home or, alternatively, should a covenant be interpreted in favor of the free use and enjoyment of property and against such restrictions? (2) Do restrictive covenants violate the FHA when they have a discriminatory intent, a disparate-impact (discriminatory effect) or fail to make reasonable accommodations under §3604(f)(3)(B)?

R Vague restrictive covenants should be interpreted in favor of the free use and enjoyment of property and against such restrictions contained therein; restrictive covenants which have a discriminatory effect, intent or fail to make reasonable accommodations under §3604(f)(3)(B) violate the Fair Housing Act.

A (1) Yes. Vague restrictive covenants should be interpreted in favor of the free use and enjoyment of property and against such restrictions contained therein. In this case, the restrictive covenant requires that all homes in the area be used for "single-family residence purposes." As to the part of the covenant which requires the use be that of a "residence," we note that operating the AIDS group home constitutes the residential use of property. "The controlling factor in considering whether a group of unrelated individuals living together as a single house-keeping unit constitutes a family ... is whether the residents bear the generic character of a relatively permanent functioning family unit," *Open Door Alcoholism Program, Inc. v. Board of Adjustment*. Here, much of the activities of the group home residents are communal in nature; the residents provide support and guidance for each other and together create an environment that assists them in living with AIDS. They share common meals together, shop together, provide financial help to each other and contract with off-site private healthcare workers. The Community provides clerical help to the residents, collects rent from them and enforces a strict no drinking and no drugs policy. As to the second part of the restriction; the requirement that the use be for only "single-family" purposes, we note that the residents of the home meet the single-family prerequisite. This is because the word "family" is not defined in the restrictive covenant and thus its use is, at best, ambiguous. Hence, we must interpret any ambiguity in favor of the free enjoyment of the property. (2) Yes. Restrictive covenants violate the FHA when they have a discriminatory intent, a discriminatory effect, or constitute a failure to make reasonable accommodations. Even if we were to adopt the neighbors' proposed definition of "family" to include only individuals related by blood or by law, we would still find for the Community because the restriction would violate the FHA. Although the neighbors' enforcement of the restrictive covenant was not intended to discriminate against AIDS victims, it certainly had that effect by denying housing to those afflicted with the disease. Thus, we must balance the neighbors' interest in avoiding an increase in traffic on their street against the Community's interest in providing housing to those with AIDS under their care. We conclude that the FHA factors weigh in favor of the Community. This is of particular importance when we consider the strong public policy favoring the placement of the disabled in congregate (involving a group) and ordinary community living environments. Lastly, we hold that plaintiffs failed to provide reasonable accommodations to those members of the group home, as mandated by the FHA. Here, "reasonable accommodations" would have been not to seek enforcement of the covenant. The ruling of the trial court is reversed and the injunction issued is vacated.

C Vague restrictive covenants should be interpreted in favor of the free use and enjoyment of property and against such restrictions contained therein; restrictive covenants which have a discriminatory effect, intent or fail to make reasonable accommodations under §3604(f)(3)(B) violate the Fair Housing Act.

Shelley v. Kraemer

334 U.S. 1 (1948)

FACTS

On February 16, 1911, 30 out of 39 owners of property along both sides of Labadie Avenue in St. Louis entered into a restrictive covenant which provided that, for the next 50 years after the date of the signing, no part of any of the property was to be used or occupied "by any person, not of the Caucasian race, it being intended hereby to restrict the use of said property for said period o time against the occupancy by people of the Negro or Mongolian race." These 30 title holders owned 47 out of a total of 57 parcels of land in the community. On August 11, 1945, the Shelleys (plaintiffs), who were African-Americans, received a warranty deed for the parcel in question from one Fitzgerald. The record indicates that the Shelleys had no actual knowledge of the restrictive covenant at the time of their purchase. On October 9, 1945, Kraemer and his neighbors, all of whom were bound by the covenant, brought an action to enjoin the Shelleys from taking possession of their newly purchased land and requested that a judgment be entered by the court divesting the Shelleys of their title and revesting title in one Shackelford or some other [non African-American] person. The Missouri Supreme Court directed the trial court to grant relief for Plaintiff Kramer and the other owners.

I Can a racially restrictive covenant be judicially enforced?

R Judicial enforcement of a racially restrictive covenant constitutes discriminatory state action, and is therefore prohibited by the Equal Protection Clause of the Fourteenth Amendment.

A We hold that in granting judicial enforcement of the restrictive agreements in these cases, the States have denied petitioners the equal protection of the laws and that, therefore, the action of the state courts cannot stand. We find support for this position in the Equal Protection Clause of the 14th Amendment which prohibits judicial enforcement by state courts of restrictive covenants based on race. We further note that freedom from discrimination by the States in the enjoyment of property rights was among the basic objectives sought to be effectuated by the framers of the 14th Amendment. That such discrimination has occurred in these cases is clear. Because of the race or color of these petitioners they have been denied rights of ownership or occupancy enjoyed as a matter of course by other citizens of different race or color. The Fourteenth Amendment declares "that all persons, whether colored or white, shall stand equal before the laws of the States, and, in regard to the colored race, for whose protection the amendment was primarily designed, that no discrimination shall be made against them by law because of their color." Had the restrictions enforced by the instant covenant been imposed by a statute or an ordinance, they would certainly be found unconstitutional. But because it is the product of a private action, not State action, the covenant by itself does not violate the 14th Amendment and thus remains constitutional. However, the covenant here was held out for judicial enforcement by the state courts. Consequently, where there is official action by state courts and judicial officers, the State is implicated because these officials are regarded as actors of the State, acting in an official, authorized capacity. Actions regarding the 14th Amendment follow a similar thread of reasoning and legal application. In the instant case, the record clearly shows that the Shelleys were willing and able buyers of the property in question and that Fitzgerald was a motivated seller. Were it not for the intercession of the Missouri State courts, the Shelleys would have been free to possess and enjoy their property. Although the racial covenant was first defined by private contract, the State must comply with the requirements of the 14th Amendment because of its action in judicially enforcing the covenant which we hold violated the Amendment.

C Judicial enforcement of a racially restrictive covenant constitutes discriminatory state action, and is therefore prohibited by the Equal Protection Clause of the Fourteenth Amendment. Judgment reversed.

TERMINATION OF COVENANTS

Western Land Co. v. Truskolaski

(1972) 88 Nev. 200, 495 P.2d 624

FACTS

In 1941, Plaintiff-Appellant Western Land Company subdivided a 40 acre development outside the city limits of Reno and subjected the lots to restrictive covenants which limited them to single-family dwellings and prohibited commercial businesses of any kind. The land around the subdivision was put mainly to residential and agricultural use, with very little commercial development. In 1941, the City of Reno had a population of about 20,000 people. By 1961, Plumb Lane, now a major thoroughfare, had expanded eastward becoming the main east-west artery through the southern part of the city. By 1969, Reno's population grew to about 95,100 people and the Lakeside Plaza Shopping Center, a major commercial enterprise, had been built across from the eastern end of the subdivision. Within its vicinity, a supermarket, butcher shop, hardware store, beauty shop and dress shop were constructed. Despite this commercial progress, the traffic density within the subdivision remained fairly low. The homeowners believed that this low level of traffic resulted in a safe environment for children playing in the area. Defendants-Respondents (the homeowners of the Southland Heights subdivision in southwest Reno) brought suit in district court to enjoin Plaintiff-Appellant Western land Co. from constructing a shopping center on a 3.5 acre parcel within the subdivision. The district court held that the restrictive covenants were still enforceable and enjoined the Western land Co. from constructing the supermarket. Western appealed.

I Can a restrictive covenant for a residential subdivision be terminated when the residential character of the neighboring area has changed but the owners therein still want enforcement of the covenant?

R A restrictive covenant for a residential subdivision cannot be terminated as long as the object and purpose of the restrictions has not been thwarted and enforcement of the covenant remains of substantial value to the landowners within the subdivision.

A A restrictive covenant for a residential subdivision cannot be terminated as long as object and purpose of the restrictions has not been thwarted and enforcement of the covenant remains of substantial value to the landowners within the subdivision. The record clearly indicates that the subdivision is still suitable for residential living in spite of the commercial changes in the area and that the covenant's restrictions remain of significant value to the landowners. Specifically, the low traffic density has provided a safe environment for children playing in the area which the landowners absolutely regard as important. Thus, the children's safety would probably be adversely affected if the added traffic were allowed to pass through the area. Appellant Western Land directs our attention to the Reno City Council's goal of rezoning the area for commercial use. However, we remain unconvinced. The City Council's intent to rezone does not prove that the property is more suited for commercial use than residential use; only that they wish it to be used commercially. Judgment affirmed.

C A restrictive covenant for a residential subdivision cannot be terminated as long as the object and purpose of the restrictions has not been thwarted and enforcement of the covenant remains of substantial value to the landowners.

Rick v. West

(1962) 34 Misc. 2d 1002, 228 N.Y.S.2d 195

FACTS

Plaintiff Chester Rick owned and subdivided 62 acres of vacant land in 1946 which included covenants that restricted the land to single-family dwellings. In 1956, plaintiff sold a one half-acre lot to Defendant Catherine West whereupon she built a house. In 1957, the land was zoned for residential use. Thereafter, plaintiff contracted for the sale of 45 acres to an industrialist, the sale being conditioned on the track being rezoned for industrial use. Even though the 45 acres was rezoned, the sale fell through. The sale failed as a direct result of defendant refusing to release the covenant. Plaintiff sold only a few of the lots, but conveyed the remaining land to the other lot owners. Again, in 1961, plaintiff tried to sell 15 acres of the track to Peekskill Hospital, but the defendant yet again refused to consent to the release of the covenant. Plaintiff sued, claiming the covenant was no longer enforceable because of a change in conditions. The trial court held for the defendant stating that there was no evidence of any substantial change in the character of the neighborhood. The plaintiffs appealed.

I Should a restrictive covenant still be enforced when only one landowner in a subdivision refuses to consent to the release of the covenant?

R The law respects and protects the rights of even a single landowner in a subdivision under a restrictive covenant who insists upon adherence to the covenant even when other owners desire and consent to its release.

A Any landowner in any subdivision under a restrictive covenant has the right to insist upon adherence to the covenant even when the other owners do not. Plaintiff owned the land in question free of all encumbrances in 1946. It was his right to do what he wished with the property. He elected to transform this land into a residential development and created certain restrictions on the lots to promote their sale. When defendant bought her lot, she relied upon those restrictions as part of sale process and she has the right to continue relying on them. We turn first to the potential advantages of having a hospital on the property. A balancing of equities approach is irrelevant here and any application weighing the benefit of a hospital on the land is immaterial. The record indicates that Defendant West is the only covenantee in opposition to releasing the covenant; however, this fact does not extinguish her right to have it fully enforced as she is just as worthy of our protection as any other. West simply insists upon adherence to covenant, which is as binding today as it was when she purchased the burdened land in 1956. Her steadfast refusal to release the covenant, stemming from her approval of the covenant as it presently exists, ought to be protected.

C The law respects and protects the rights of even a single landowner in a subdivision under a restrictive covenant who insists upon adherence to the covenant even when other owners desire and consent to its release. Judgment affirmed.

Pocono Springs Civic Association, Inc. v. MacKenzie
446 Pa. Super. 445, 667 A.2d 233 (Penn. 1995)

FACTS

Defendants-Appellants Joseph and Doris MacKenzie purchased a lot in the Pocono Springs housing development in October, 1969. By 1987, plaintiffs decided to sell the lot which was still vacant. An offer for the purchase of the lot later fell through because it had been conditioned upon the property being suited for an on-lot sewage system which it was not. Thereafter, the defendants took several actions evidencing their intent to abandon the property including an attempt to turn the lot over to the appellee, which was declined; their mailed notarized statement to "all interested parties" expressing their desire to abandon the lot; and an assertion that they neither visited the lot nor utilized the development's services since 1986. Defendant also stopped paying all Association fees. Plaintiff-Appellant Pocono Springs Civic Association sued the defendants for payment. At trial, defendants defended on the grounds that they had abandoned the lot. The trial court rejected the defendants' abandonment defense and granted summary judgment in favor of the Association. Defendants appealed.

I Can an owner of real property successfully abandon his property when he still possesses perfect title?

R Where the owner still holds title in fee simple absolute and has not relinquished his rights, title, claim and possession to the property, that property cannot be considered abandoned.

A We turn first to appellants' argument and the issue of intent. Appellants' claim that the trial court erred in granting summary judgment because whether they abandoned their property should be a question of intent. We reject this argument noting that appellants' intent is irrelevant to this legal analysis. The law in our state is clear: if owner still possesses perfect title, real property held in Pennsylvania cannot be considered "abandoned." Abandoned property is that property "to which an owner has voluntarily relinquished all right, title, claim and possession with the intent of terminating his ownership, but without vesting it in any other person, and with the intention of not reclaiming further possession or resuming ownership." The evidence clearly indicates that defendants have not surrendered their rights or title to their lot and remain the owners of the land in fee simple. Neither the title nor the deed has been sold or transferred to another. Thus, we need not go any further. As a matter of law, the defendants' defense must fail. Notwithstanding appellants' argument to the contrary, they have not abandoned the property.

C Where the owner still holds title in fee simple absolute and has not relinquished his rights, title, claim and possession to the property, that property cannot be considered abandoned.

Affirmed.

COMMON INTEREST COMMUNITIES

Nahrstedt v. Lakeside Village Condo Assn., Inc.

(1922) 11 Cal. Rptr. 2d 299, hearing granted by Calif. Sup. Ct.

FACTS

Plaintiff Natore Nahrstedt, an owner of three cats, sued her condominium complex (Association) to prevent the homeowners association from enforcing a restriction against house pets. The relevant restriction provided that "no animals, which shall mean dogs and cats, ...shall be kept in any unit" and that "the Association shall have the right to prohibit maintenance of any pet, which constitutes, in the opinion of the Board of Directors of the Homeowners Association, a nuisance to any other owner." The Association has supposedly harassed her by levying fines penalizing her for keeping the cats in her apartment. Plaintiff sued the Association, its officers and two employees (1) requesting the trial court to invalidate the assessments and declare them "unreasonable" as applied to indoor cats; (2) that she not be compelled to pay the fines; and that (3) the restriction was "unreasonable" under the Civil Code §1354. The Association demurred to the complaint and the trial court sustained the demurrers on all causes of action without leave to amend. On the Association's petition, we grant review of the relevant issue(s).

I Is a pet restriction that is contained in the recorded declaration of a condominium complex enforceable against a homeowner?

R The reasonableness or unreasonableness of the restrictions on pets should be decided by a trial court after the evidence is heard and applied to the common interest of the development as a whole, not by the facts that are specific to the complaining landowner.

A Under our holding today, the reasonableness or unreasonableness of the restrictions on pets should be decided by a trial court after the evidence is heard and applied to the common interest of the development as a whole, not by the facts that are specific to the complaining landowner. The Association maintained that the restriction against pets is reasonable and thus enforceable because it protects the Association from frequent litigation against those whose animals who do cause harm. To address this issue, the Court of Appeal relied on *Bernardo Villas Manag. Corp. v. Black* (provision allowing parking of trucks only for loading and unloading held unreasonable when applied to clean noncommercial pickup trucks) and the court's holding in *Portola Hills Community Assoc. v. James* (ban on satellite dishes in planned community held unreasonable when dish not visible to other community residents) which is to judge situations on their own specific facts. However, applying the law of these two cases to the instant facts, the Court of Appeal failed to consider the rules governing equitable servitudes when it held that Nahrstedt's complaint stated a cause of action for declaratory relief. This is because both *Bernardo Villas* and *Portola Hills* failed to evaluate the deferential standards of equitable servitude law, and, accordingly, we reject both holdings. When applying equitable servitude law, a court's determination as to whether a restriction is "unreasonable" under §1354, and thus <u>not</u> enforceable, should focus is on the restriction's effect on the project as a whole, not on an individual homeowner. Thus, when a restriction exists and is contained in the declaration of the common interest development and has properly been recorded with the County Clerk, the restriction is presumed reasonable and will thus be enforced uniformly against all residents in the development unless the restriction is (1) arbitrary; (2) imposes a burden on the land it affects or (3) violates some fundamental public policy. Thus, we conclude as a mater of law, that the recorded restriction of the Lakeside Village Condominium Association is not arbitrary and is rationally related to the health, sanitation and safety concerns legitimately held by residents of a multiunit condominium. We note that plaintiff's complaint does not allege any facts that could possibly support a finding that the burden of the restriction is disproportionate to its benefit. We are unaware of any public policy that would favor keeping pets in a condominium and add that there is no state or federal law that confers a general right to keep household pets in a condominium, coop or other residential development. Moreover, for many homeowners, the pet restriction may have been an inducement to buy into the development. Thus, we reverse the judgment of the Court of Appeal and remand this case for further proceedings consistent with the views expressed in this opinion.

C The reasonableness or unreasonableness of the restrictions on pets should be decided by a trial court after the evidence is heard and applied to the common interest of the development as a whole, not by the facts that are specific to the complaining landowner.

VIII. ADVERSE POSSESSION

Adverse possession is a method of acquiring title to property by possession for a statutory period of time if certain elements are met. The elements of adverse possession are:

A. Hostile

The adverse possessor must be hostile in his possession of the land. This means that the adverse possessor must not have the permission of the true owner to use the land.

B. Actual

The possession of the land by the adverse possessor must be consistent with the normal use of the land. For example, if the land is used seasonally, seasonal use of the land by the adverse possessor satisfies the element.

C. Open and Notorious

The open and notorious element is satisfied when the adverse possessor puts the true owner on notice that a trespass is occurring on the true owner's land.

D. Exclusive

The adverse possessor is not sharing the land with the true owner or the public.

E. Continuous for the Statutory Period of Time

Each jurisdiction has a statutory period of time for which an adverse possessor must occupy the land of the true owner for the element to be satisfied. At common law, the statutory period of time is twenty years. However, there need not be continuous possession by the same person. The period of adverse possession of one possessor could be "tacked" to the period of adverse possession of another possessor when there is privity between the two.

ADVERSE POSSESSION OF CHATTELS

O'Keeffe v. Snyder

(1980) 83 N.J. 478; 416 A.2d 862

FACTS

This is an appeal from an order of the Appellate Division granting summary judgment to Plaintiff Georgia O'Keeffe against Defendant Barry Snyder, d/b/a Princeton Gallery of Fine Arts, for replevin of three paintings by O'Keeffe. In 1946 three paintings by O'Keeffe (plaintiff) were stolen from a New York art gallery, operated by her late husband, the famous photographer Alfred Stieglitz. Plaintiff did not report the theft to the police. O'Keeffe explains that she did not pursue her efforts to find the paintings because she was settling her deceased husband's estate. She retained the services of Doris Bry to help settle the estate. Finally, in 1972 O'Keeffe authorized Bry to report the theft to the Art Dealers Association of America. In 1976, O'Keeffe discovered that Ulrich A. Frank had sold her paintings to Defendant Snyder. Frank claimed to have acquired the paintings from his father and did not know how his father acquired the paintings, but he recalled seeing them in his father's house as early as 1941 or 1943. However, Snyder's claim is inconsistent with O'Keeffe's recollection of the theft. Nevertheless, for the purposes of this appeal, defendant concedes that the paintings were, in fact, stolen. Frank declares at least 30 years continuous possession of the paintings from his father thus claiming title by adverse possession.

I When did O'Keeffe's cause of action accrue, on the date of the alleged theft, March, 1946, or more than six years before the date of suit via adverse possession by the defendant or his predecessors?

R The statute of limitations is tolled (suspended) if the owner of stolen chattel makes a thorough effort to locate and recover the lost chattel.

A We hold that the discovery rule applies to an action for replevin of a painting. The discovery rule, as it applies to this case, states that upon discovery of the theft, the statute of limitations is tolled (suspended) if the true owner of the chattels makes diligent efforts to locate and recover the lost chattels. "Diligent efforts" include reporting the theft to the police or registering the chattels with a registry so as to notify potential buyers that the chattels may be stolen. If O'Keeffe in fact made such diligent efforts, her cause of action would accrue when she first knew, or reasonably should have known through the exercise of due diligence of the cause of action, including the identity of the possessor of the paintings. In determining whether a O'Keeffe is entitled to the benefit of discovery rule, the trial court should consider, among other things, the following issues: (1) whether O'Keeffe used to diligence to recover the paintings at that time of the alleged theft and thereafter come; (2) whether at the time of the alleged theft there was an effective method, other than talking to her colleagues, for O'Keeffe to alert the art world; and (3) whether registering paintings with the Art Dealers Association of America Inc. or any other organization would put a reasonably prudent purchaser of art on constructive notice that someone other than the possessor was the true owner. However, if Frank acquired voidable title from his father, who may have been a thief, Frank still has the power to transfer good title to a good-faith purchaser under the U.C.C. If defendant Synder was not a good faith purchaser, or if Frank did not have voidable title, the defendant may still acquire title by adverse possession. However, as we have already mentioned, in certain situations, the statute of limitations may be tolled to avoid harsh results. Consequently, we reverse the judgment of the Appellate Division in favor of O'Keefee and remand the matter for trial for a finding of whether O'Keefe used diligence in discovering who is lost the paintings.

C The statute of limitations is tolled (suspended) if the owner of stolen chattel makes a thorough effort to locate and recover the lost chattel. Reversed and remanded.

IX. CONVEYANCE OF TITLE OF REAL PROPERTY

The Deed

A deed is a written instrument by which land is conveyed.

1. **The Elements of a Deed**
   The statute of frauds requires that contracts for the sale of land be in writing and signed by the grantor. However, under the **Part Performance Doctrine** (discussed later) an oral contract for the sale of land may be specifically enforced if certain conditions are met. The elements of a deed are as follows:

   a. Signature of the grantor
   b. Consideration
   c. Identification of the buyer and seller
   d. Description of the property
   e. Grantor's intent to delivery the deed
   f. Acceptance of the deed by grantee

2. **Types of Deeds**

   a. Warranty Deed
   A warranty deed is a deed that expressly guarantees the grantor's good clear title and contains covenants concerning the quality of title including:

   - **Warrantees of Seisin** - grantor owns the property he purports to convey.
   - **Quiet Enjoyment** - grantee will not be disturbed in his possession of the property.
   - **Right to Convey** - grantor has the right to convey the property he purports to convey.
   - **Freedom of Encumbrances** - the property is free from any liens.
   - **Defense of Title Against all Claims** - the grantor will perform whatever acts may be

reasonably necessary to protect the grantee's title.

b. **Special Warranty Deed**
A special warranty deed is a deed in which the grantor covenants to warrant and defend the title against claims and demands of only the grantor and all persons claiming by and under him.

c. **Quitclaim Deed**
A quitclaim deed is a deed that conveys a grantor's complete interest or claim in real property but neither warrants nor professes that the title is valid.

Part Performance

Under the part performance doctrine, an oral contract to sell land is enforceable in equity despite the statute of frauds (requirement of a writing). Part performance can come in many forms. However, the acts that are recognized by the courts for part performance are the following:

Payment of all or part of the purchase price, and <u>either</u>:

a. delivery of possession of the land to the vendee; or
b. via the construction of permanent and valuable improvements by the vendee.

C. Equitable Conversion

Equitable conversion is the doctrine that treats interests

in land as if they have already been converted into personal property. This doctrine states that the purchaser is the equitable owner of the land and not the vendor, even though he may still have legal title to the land. Therefore, if a piece of property is destroyed during the executory period (time between when the contract is signed and the closing) but before the closing, and neither party is at fault, the risk of loss is on the buyer and he must pay the contract price.

However, a minority of states follow the **Uniform Vendor and Purchaser Risk Act** (UVPRA). Under this Act, the risk of loss is on the seller during the executory period unless the buyer has actually taken possession of the property or has legal title to the property at the time the property is destroyed.

D. Marketable Title

Land contracts come with an implied assurance of marketable title. If, however, the vendor fails to deliver marketable title, the vendee may rescind the contract.

The vendor is only obligated to tender marketable title on the closing date and the purchaser may not rescind the contract before the time of performance. If the buyer becomes aware that that the title is unmarketable, he must notify the seller and allow him (the seller) reasonable time to cure the defect even if it extends past the closing date. If the seller fails to cure the defect within a reasonable time, the buyer may rescind the contract. The buyer may also sue for damages for the breach or specific performance including a reduction in the purchase price to reflect the defect in title.

The following are defects that render title unmarketable:

1. Encumbrances
2. Encroachments
3. Easements
4. Mortgages or liens
5. Restrictive Covenants
6. Land subject to claims of adverse possession

E. Recording Statutes

Recording statutes provide a means of giving constructive notice of ownership of a piece of property by recording them with the county clerk's office. Recording statutes apply to deeds as well as mortgages and are only applicable when two parties each claim to be the record titleholder of a particular piece of property. There are three types of recording statutes depending on the jurisdiction:

1. Race Statutes

Under this statute the first party to record holds the title to the piece of property.

2. Notice Statutes

Under this statute, the last bona fide purchaser of the property for value has title to the piece of property. A bona fide purchaser for value is a person who tenders value for property and is without notice that there is a previous buyer of the same piece of property.

3. Race Notice Statutes

Under this statute, the first bona fide purchaser for value who records has title to the piece of property.

THE STATUTE OF FRAUDS

Hickey v. Green

Appeals Court of Massachusetts, 1982 14 Mass. App. Ct. 671, 442 N.E. 2d 37

FACTS

Mrs. Gladys Green owned a lot (Lot S) in Plymouth, Massachusetts. On July 11 and 12, 1980, plaintiffs (the Hickeys) orally agreed to purchase

Lot S from Mrs. Green (defendant) for $15,000 and on July 12, Mrs. Green accepted a deposit check for $500. The Payee name was left blank because the Hickeys were uncertain whether Mrs. Green or her brother was to receive the check. Defendant held the check, did not fill in a payee's name and neither cashed nor endorsed it. On July 24, defendant informed the Hickeys that she no longer intended to sell her property to them but had decided to sell it to another buyer for $16,000. Hickey told defendant that he had already sold his home and offered to match the other offer, but defendant still refused to sell to them. Plaintiffs sued, seeking specific performance of the oral agreement. Defendant argues that the relief requested is barred by the Statute of Frauds. The trial court granted specific performance and Mrs. Green appealed.

I Can specific performance be granted to party where an oral contract for the transfer of land exists, notwithstanding the Statute of Frauds, if the party seeking enforcement has substantially relied on the oral agreement?

R An oral agreement for the transfer of land is sufficient to overcome the Statute of Frauds requirement of a writing when there is an oral promise, partial payment and an act (taking possession) made in reliance thereof is evidenced.

A Restatement (Second) of Contracts, §129 provides that notwithstanding a failure to comply with the Statute of Frauds, the party seeking enforcement of the contract for the transfer of an interest in land may nonetheless enforce the contract if he reasonably relied on it and changed his position in reliance thereof such that injustice to him can only be avoided by specific enforcement. An oral promise coupled with part performance is sufficient to overcome the Statute of Frauds. While payment of the purchase price alone is not sufficient to constitute part performance, payment and subsequent possession of the property by the buyer is. In the instant case, the evidence reveals that both parties intended to close the sale of Lot S quickly. For this reason, plaintiffs attempted to sell their house quickly, without seeking the guarantees a written contract would have provided. Furthermore, legal counsel was not used by either side, suggesting the parties did not intend to formalize their agreement. The Hickeys acceptance and endorsement of a deposit for the sale their house would probably have exposed them to expensive litigation had they attempted to avoid the sale of their home. The key piece of evidence here is that Mrs. Green did not deny that an oral agreement existed between the parties. This is important because it shows both the elements of injustice and that the Hickeys reliance on the oral contract was both reasonable and appropriate.

C An oral agreement for the transfer of land can overcome the Statute of Frauds when there is an oral promise, partial payment and an act (taking possession) made in reliance thereof is evidenced. Judgment affirmed.

MARKETABLE TITLE

Lohmeyer v. Bower

Supreme Court of Kansas, 1951 170 Kan. 442, 227 P. 2d 102

FACTS

Plaintiff Dr. K.L. Lohmeyer entered into a contract to purchase Lot 37 from Defendant Bower in Berkeley Hills in the City of Emporia. The contract provided that the Bowers (defendant) would convey title by Warranty Deed; that is, the conveyance was subject to the defendant producing a merchantable title showing it was free and clear of all encumbrances. In addition, Lot 37 was subject to a restrictive covenant whereby any house erected on it was to be two stories in height. Additionally, a local municipal ordinance provided that no house was to be less than three feet from any side or rear lot line. The house on Lot 37 violated both restrictions; it was one story in height and was located within 18 inches of the north lot line of the property. Plaintiff Lohmeyer brought suit to rescind the contract and demanded the return of his money. The Bowers answered, contesting his right to rescind the contract and cross-complained for specific performance. The trial court rendered judgment for the Bowers and plaintiff appealed.

I Is title rendered unmarketable when the property is subject to encumbrances, such as the violation of an ordinance or other burdens placed on it?

R If title to real property does not expose the buyer to litigation, it is marketable title.

A *Peating v. Baird* clarifies what constitutes marketable title. The court held in that case that a marketable title to real estate is one which is free for reasonable doubt, and a title is doubtful and unmarketable if it exposes the party holding it to the hazard of litigation. To render the title to real estate unmarketable, the defect of which the purchaser complaints must be of a substantial character and one from which he may suffer injury. Mere material defects, which do not diminish the quality, value, or quantity of the property contracted for do not constitute valid grounds upon which the purchaser may reject the title. That being said, a buyer may ordinary not rescind a contract to purchase land where the encumbrance on the title is the result of a municipal ordinance; but may rescind a contract based on the existence of private covenants. Here, the plaintiff agreed to accept private covenants. Thus, his case is premised on the fact that the house on Lot 37 violates certain restrictions, leaving him open to litigation. Property that violative of both a private covenants and municipal requirements will expose plaintiff to litigation. The contract provides that the defendant is entitled to a reasonable amount of time to correct the restrictions. The lot line problem may be corrected through the purchase of more land but requiring the addition of a second-floor onto the house is simply unreasonable. Accordingly, the judgment is reversed with instructions to the trial court to cancel and set aside the contract.

C If title to real property does not expose the buyer to litigation, it is marketable title.

Conklin v. Davi

Supreme Court of new Jersey, 1978 76 N.J. 468, 388 A.2d 598

FACTS

Defendant Conklin contracted to sell residential property in Ridgewood, N.J. to Plaintiff Davi. Plaintiff refused to complete the sale, alleging various defects in title and material misrepresentations; specifically that defendant's claim to title was based on adverse possession. At the outset, defendant sued for specific performance and plaintiff counterclaimed for rescission of the contract. However, before trial, the plaintiff dropped his claim for specific performance and the case proceeded solely as an action on the counterclaim of the defendants-purchasers (the rescission action). The rescission claim asserted that defendant's claim of ownership (based on adverse possession) rendered the title unmarketable absent a deed or action to quiet title. At the close of the plaintiff's case, the trial court granted defendant's motion for summary judgment. Plaintiff appealed, and the Appellate Court reversed the trial court's judgment and entered a judgment in favor of the plaintiff. The Appellate Court did not remand the case.

I Under New Jersey Property Law, when a parcel of land is held by adverse possession is the title unmarketable, thus voiding the contract?

R In a suit where a buyer seeking rescission has shown that record title is held by adverse possession, the burden shifts to the seller to establish his title by adverse possession. Thus, the seller will prevail if the court <u>ultimately</u> finds the title to be marketable.

A When a prospective seller's title is grounded upon adverse possession or contains some apparent flaw of record, the seller may take steps to perfect the record title (e.g., quiet title, rectify outstanding encumbrances). Thus, a contract for the sale of real property does not require a valid title of record; only that title be marketable or insurable. In this case, at trial, testimony was proffered that the insurance company would have insured the property and a marketable title guarantees that buyers are free from unreasonable doubt about their property. It does not require a guarantee that the title is flawless. While summary judgment granted by the trial court was in error, the appellate court should have granted the defendant a *de novo* trial. This would have allowed the defendant an opportunity to demonstrate to the court that title was marketable. The marketability of title need only be proven at trial; there is no requirement that it be proven before trial. Lastly, an action to quiet title is not necessary to demonstrate marketability in the case of adverse possession. Although we agree with the Appellate Court that the trial court erred in granting the motion; we think that its entry of a judgment in plaintiff's favor was equally erroneous. Accordingly, we order a new trial.

C The seller will prevail if in an action for specific performance, if, at the conclusion of the suit, the court finds title to be marketable, even if it was alleged to be unmarketable before trial. Judgment entered in favor of the plaintiff is reversed and the cause remanded for a new trial.

THE DUTY TO DISCLOSE DEFECTS

Stambovsky v. Ackley

N.Y. Supr. Ct., Appellate Div., First Dept., 1991 169 A.D.2d 254, 572 N.Y.S.2d 672

FACTS

Plaintiff-Appellant Stambovsky, a resident of New York City, bought the house of Defendant-Respondent Ackley in the Village of Nyack. Thereafter, plaintiff discovered that the house was haunted and reputed to be possessed by poltergeists; reportedly seen by the seller and her family over the last nine years. Defendant had, for some time, fostered the house's reputation by reporting the presence of ghosts to the local newspaper and by including the home in a walking tour of Nyack. Plaintiff was not told the house was haunted. Plaintiff commenced an action in the Supreme Court of New York for rescission of the contract, but the trial court dismissed the complaint holding that the plaintiff had no remedy at law and because of the doctrine of caveat emptor ("let the buyer beware") was applicable. Plaintiff appealed.

I Under New York property law, can the nondisclosure of a material fact(s) which adversely affect(s) the value of land be the basis for the rescission of the sales contract, where the buyer has acted reasonably and prudently and where the seller has created the material condition?

R Failure to disclose a condition forms the basis of rescission where (1) a seller has created the condition which materially impairs the value of the contract; (2) the condition is uniquely within the knowledge of the seller; and (3) the condition is unlikely to be discovered by a prudent buyer.

A We do not decide here whether the house was, in fact, haunted. Rather, we look to the impact of the folklore that the house was haunted as disseminated and parlayed by the defendant. Consequently, the defendant cannot deny the existence of the spirits and that the house is, as a matter of law, possessed. Defendant fostered the house's reputation by various means. This proactive fostering materially impacted the house's marketability. The doctrine of caveat emptor is applicable where the buyer has an equal opportunity to discover details about the house which he is buying. But it is easier said than done for a future buyer to order an inspection for the supernatural and we do not want to create a precedent that suggests that buyers should do so. We acknowledge that a conventional means of disproving the doctrine was to show that the seller affirmatively concealed a material fact. And while defendant did not actively conceal the existence of poltergeists, she took unjust advantage of the plaintiff's lack of knowledge of the folklore of the Village of Nyack. This is true even though the seller's agent (the real estate broker) was not compelled by law to disclose the existence of the spirits. We therefore hold, in consideration of all of the above, that to enforce this contract would be to offend society's notion of fairness and equity and permit the seller to take unfair advantage of the buyer's ignorance.

C Failure to disclose a condition forms the basis of rescission where (1) a seller has created the condition which materially impairs the value of the contract; (2) the condition is only within the knowledge of the seller; and (3) the condition is unlikely to be discovered by a prudent buyer. Judgment modified.

Johnson v. Davis

Supreme Court of Florida, 1985 480 So. 2d 625

FACTS

The Johnsons (defendant) contracted to sell their home to the Davises (plaintiff) for $310,000. Defendant knew that the roof leaked, but they affirmatively represented to plaintiff that it did not. Several days later, plaintiff discovered water "gushing" into the home from around the windows and from the ceiling in two rooms as the result of heavy rain. Plaintiff sued to rescind the contract and recover their deposit. The court held that there was misrepresentation on the part of the defendant-sellers entitling the Davises to rescind the sales contract.

I Where a seller is aware of a material fact of which the buyer is unaware, does the seller have an affirmative duty to disclose that fact?

R Where a material fact(s) affects the value of the property and those facts are not known or readily observable to the buyer, a seller of real property is under a duty to disclose such material facts to the prospective buyer.

A The Johnsons' fraudulent concealment and affirmative representation that the roof was undamaged was a material misrepresentation thus entitling the Davises to rescission of the sales contract. This is true even if defendant had not positively lied – the plaintiff should still be free to recover. Thus, where the failure to disclose a material fact was intended to provoke a phony belief, the difference between actual "concealment" and an "affirmative misrepresentation" is immaterial. The application of the doctrine of caveat emptor, which relieves a seller from liability for concealing material facts, is inapplicable here as it is out of step with modern times and does not conform to current notions of justice, equity and fair dealing. We do not allow a seller to take advantage of a buyer's ignorance. Thus, where the seller has information that adversely impacts the value of the property and where that information is concealed from the buyer, the seller has an affirmative duty to disclose those material facts.

C Where a material fact(s) affects the value of the property and those facts are not known or readily apparent to the buyer, a seller of real property is under a duty to disclose such material facts to the prospective buyer. Judgment affirmed.

THE IMPLIED WARRANTY OF TITLE

Lempke v. Dagenais

Supreme Court of New Hampshire, 1988 130 N.H. 782, 547 A.2d 290

FACTS

In 1977 Plaintiffs Elaine and Larry Lempke's predecessors in title contracted with Defendant Dagenais to build a garage on their property. In April 1978, six months after the garage's construction, plaintiffs bought the property. Shortly after they purchased the property, the plaintiffs noticed structural defects in the garage's construction: the roof line was uneven and the roof trusses were bowing out. Fearing a cave-in, the plaintiffs contacted the defendant and asked him to repair the defects; the defendant initially agreed to do so but never completed the repairs. Plaintiffs sued defendant under the theory of implied warranty of workmanlike quality for latent defects which caused economic loss, absence of privity of contract, negligence and breach of assigned to contractual rights.

I Where there is a breach of implied warranty of workmanship and quality by a builder, does a successor in title have a cause of action against that builder?

R Privity of contract is not needed for a subsequent purchaser to sue a builder or contractor under an implied warranty theory for latent defects, which manifests within a reasonable time after purchase, and which caused economic harm.

A We hold that privity of contract is not necessary for a subsequent purchaser to sue a builder or contractor under an implied warranty theory for latent defects, which manifests within a reasonable time after purchase, and which caused economic harm. The lower court relied on the holding of *Ellis v. Morris* which held that a successor in interest could not recover for economic loss for the implied warranty of workmanship and good-quality (absence privity of contract) for its opinion. Legal experts have long debated whether the implied warranty theory is grounded in tort, in contract or is a hybrid of both. Nevertheless, the implied warranty theory is a public policy doctrine that exists apart from any legal theory or agreement between the parties. Its purpose is to protect buyers from latent flaws in their homes. To that end, we hold that the privity prerequisite of the implied warranty of quality should be discarded where an ensuing buyer suffers economic loss from a latent defect. Not to do so would leave innocent buyers without a remedy. We stress, however, that there are limitations on our holding. Builders are not insurers. Their duty is to perform competently, according to acceptable industry standards. Moreover, the extension of the doctrine is limited to *latent* defects, where the buyer did not know of and should not have known of the defect upon reasonable inspection. Lastly, the extension is limited to a reasonable period of time where the plaintiff shoulders the burden of proving the defect was the result of the builder's inferior work. Accordingly, we reverse and remand.

C Privity of contract is not needed for a subsequent purchaser to sue a builder or contractor under an implied warranty theory for latent defects, which manifests within a reasonable time after purchase, and which caused economic harm.

THE DEED: WARRANTIES OF TITLE

Brown v. Lober

75 Ill. 2d 547, 389 N.E.2d 1188 (1979)

FACTS

In 1947 the owner of 80 acres of land conveyed it to William and Faith Bost while reserving a 2/3 interest in the mineral rights (the Bosts received the remaining 1/3 mineral interest). In 1957, the Bosts conveyed the 80 acre tract to Plaintiff James R. Brown and his wife by a general warranty deed with no exceptions. In 1974, the plaintiffs contracted to sell their mineral rights to Consolidated Coal Company for $6,000. Consolidated Coal, renegotiated the contract to provide for a payment of only $2000 to the Browns after learning that the Browns possessed only 1/3 of the mineral rights. The prior grantor never made any attempt whatsoever to exercise his mineral rights to the land. The 10 year statute of limitations barred a suit on the present covenants so the Browns sued the defendant, the executor of the Bost's estate, for $4000 in damages for the breach of the covenant of quiet enjoyment. The trial court held for the defendant, but the Appellate Court reversed.

I Did the plaintiffs present facts sufficient to show that there was constructive eviction on the part of the defendants which would create a breach of the covenant of quiet enjoyment?

R The mere fact that the plaintiffs had to modify their contract with the coal company was not enough to constitute constructive eviction necessary to sustain a breach of the covenant of quiet enjoyment; thus there is no breach of the covenant or constructive eviction where the covenantee's right of possession is not interfered with.

A A covenant of quite enjoyment can be breached by constructive eviction but there is no breach of the covenant or constructive eviction where the covenantee's right of possession is not interfered with. Our earlier decision in *Scott v. Kirkendall* (breach of covenant of quiet enjoyment of surface rights rejected because Scott could have taken possession at any time), is controlling in the instant case. There, defendant granted title to plaintiff, although others held superior title. Although *Scott* dealt with surface rights, and not with mineral rights as we see here, its logic is still relevant. In this case, no attempt was made to remove the minerals from the ground nor was anyone put on notice that the mineral interest was being exclusively used or enjoyed. Just as the surface of the land was vacant in *Scott*, so too is the mineral estate of the land in this case. Similarly, plaintiffs here could have taken peaceable possession of the estate at any time without interference from anyone. Unless plaintiffs meet opposition in exercising their right of possession, there is no breach of the covenant of quiet enjoyment. We note that there is a breach of the covenant of seisin stemming from the Bost-Brown deed, but this issue was not raised within the limitations period by the plaintiffs. Consolidated Coal's modification of the contract with the plaintiffs does not constitute a breach of the covenant of quiet enjoyment.

C A covenant of quite enjoyment can be breached by constructive eviction but there is no breach of the covenant or constructive eviction where the covenantee's right of possession is not interfered with. Reversed.

Frimberger v. Anzellotti

Appellate Court of Connecticut, 1991 25 Conn. App. 401, 594 A.2d 1029

FACTS

Defendant's brother, one DiLoreto, developed some land by building a bulkhead and filling that portion of the land which was adjacent to tidal wetlands. He then built a dwelling on the property. The land was subject to restrictive land use statutes. DiLoreto then transferred the property to Defendant Anzellotti. Thereafter, defendant sold the property to Plaintiff Frimberger, free and clear of all encumbrances, but subject to all building, building line and zoning restrictions. During the summer of 1986, plaintiff hired engineers to make repairs on the property. The engineers noted that there was a tidal wetlands violation on the property discovered stemming from the improvements to the property made by the original owner. The Department of Environmental Protection (DEP) informed plaintiff that he could submit an application to the DEP, explaining the necessity of maintaining the bulkhead. Plaintiff was not fined nor was he subjected to any sanctions for the violations by the DEP. Even so, the plaintiff sued defendant for breach of warranty against encumbrances, without submitting the application to the DEP.

I Can an alleged latent violation of a land use statute or regulation, existing on the land at the time the land was conveyed, constitute an encumbrance such that the conveyance breaches the grantor's warranty against encumbrances?

R The warranty against encumbrances can be violated by a latent violation of a restrictive land use statute or regulation.

A In *Fahmie v. Wulster* (the buyer of property sued the seller for breach of the warranty against encumbrances) the court decided that unequivocal contract provisions between the parties were the better method of protecting buyers in cases involving a breach of warranty against encumbrances. This was because, in the court's view, any extension of the warranty against encumbrances to land use violations would cause too much uncertainty in the law of conveying and title insurance because neither a title search nor a physical examination of the premises would disclose the violation. In the instant case, the DEP had taken no official action against the plaintiff. Thus, the trial court was mistaken in awarding damages based on anticipated costs because the plaintiff had not yet been exposed to any real injury. Moreover, plaintiff, an attorney and land developer, could have protected himself *before* purchasing the land by ordering a survey to guarantee compliance with the code or he could have added protective legal language in the deed to shield himself from liability for violations. Moreover, the defendant cannot be held liable for innocent misrepresentation, as the trial court held, in basing its finding on its determination that defendant breached the warranty against encumbrances. Since we have found the defendant did not breach the warranty against encumbrances, there can be no innocent misrepresentation.

C The warranty against encumbrances can be violated by a latent violation of a restrictive land use statute or regulation.

Rockafellor v. Gray

194 Iowa 1280, 191 N.W. 107 (1922)

FACTS

On October 14, 1907, 80 acres of land were conveyed to Plaintiff Rockafellor by warranty deed from one Doffing. Plaintiff additionally assumed a $500 mortgage in favor of Defendant Gray along with the conveyance. Thereafter, defendant initiated foreclosure proceedings against Duffing, which culminated in a sheriff's deed, and which was executed and delivered to Appellant Connolly on February 23, 1911. Connolly conveyed the property to Dixon. The deed contained the usual covenants of warranty, and recited consideration of $4000 which Dixon paid for the deed. Thereafter, Dixon conveyed the land to Hansen & Gregerson for $7,000. On August 15, 1918, Plaintiff Rockafellor brought suit to vacate and set aside the foreclosure sale on the grounds that the court did not obtain jurisdiction over him. On January 13, 1920, Hansen & Gregerson cross-complained against Connolly on the basis that the covenant of seisin in the Connolly-Dixon deed also applied to Hansen & Gregerson.

I Does the covenant of seisin run with the land in the State of Iowa, so that an action may be maintained by a remote grantee?

R The covenant of seisin in this jurisdiction runs with the land; is broken the instant a conveyance is delivered and then becomes a chose in action (the right to bring an action to recover debt, money or a thing) held by the covenantee in the deed. A deed given by that covenantee operates as an assignment of such chose in action to a remote grantee, who can maintain an action against the grantor in the original deed.

A Most states hold that the covenant of seisin does not run with the land; however, we reject this American Rule and adopt the English Rule. The English Rule states that the covenant of seisin does run with the land and is broken the instant the covenant conveyance is delivered. It becomes a chose action held by the covenantee in the deed which then operates as an assignment of the chose in action to a remote grantee, who can then maintain an action against the grantor in the original deed. Here, Connolly argues that because he was never in possession of the land, the covenant cannot run with the land. This is because in order for a covenant to run with the land, there must be seisin and seisin requires possession. This argument is in error because adhere to the English Rule that the covenant of seisin exists as a chose in action. We note that Connolly does not argue that Dixon was not protected by the covenant of seisin. Thus, because Dixon was protected by the covenant, he could assign the covenant as a chose in action. Therefore, Hansen & Gregerson are entitled to recovery of the consideration recited in the original Connelly-Dixon grant.

C The covenant of seisin does run with the land, and is broken the moment the conveyance is delivered, becoming a chose in action held by the covenantee. Judgment affirmed.

THE DEED: DELIVERY

Sweeney, Administratrix v. Sweeney

Supreme Court of Errors of Connecticut, 1940 126 Conn. 391, 11 A.2d 806

FACTS

Maurice Sweeney, plaintiff's intestate, deeded his farm, which included a tavern, to his brother Defendant John Sweeney so that his brother may have it in case he (Maurice) died. This deed was recorded. Maurice also protected himself in case John predeceased him by having John execute a deed transferring the property back to himself. While the first deed was recorded, the second deed was not. The second deed from John back to Maurice was accidentally destroyed in a fire. Maurice lived on the track of land which consisted of some 135 acres which he owned in East

Hampton and ran the tavern with John's limited help. Upon Maurice's death, his estranged wife (plaintiff) and the administratrix of Maurice, claimed the property by virtue of the second deed. The trial court concluded that there was no intention to make a present delivery of John's deed to Maurice and that there was no delivery and acceptance; ultimately rendering judgment for the defendant.

I Has a valid delivery been made where a deed is handed to a grantee, but the intention of the grantor is that it is to take effect only upon his (the grantor's) death?

R A deed is considered properly delivered when it is handed to grantee and is to take effect only upon the death of the grantor.

A We hold that there was a valid delivery. The deed having in effect actually delivered to Maurice, the execution of the attestation clause was *prima facie* evidence that the deed was delivered. Hence there was a rebuttable presumption that the grantee (Maurice) assented because the deed was beneficial to him. John offered nothing to rebut the claims of delivery. In fact, John himself stated that the purpose of the delivery was to allow Maurice to get the land back in the event he predeceased Maurice; and this could not occur without a valid delivery. Hence, there was a delivery. Defendant also claims that if there was a delivery, it was conditional and was not and could not be fulfilled. Yet, a conditional delivery can only occur if the grantor puts the deed into the hands of a third-party. In this case, the grantor delivered the deed to the grantee himself. Even though the evidence insinuates that the intention of the parties was to make the deed conditional, we cannot alter the rules to fit the facts. This would inevitably lead to fraud. Even though this may defeat the grantee's intent in the case at bar, it is a preferable outcome as it guards against the fabrication of evidence.

C A deed is considered properly delivered when it is handed to grantee and is to take effect only upon the death of the grantor. Judgment reverse and case remanded; a new trial is ordered.

Rosengrant v. Rosengrant

629 P.2d 800 (Okla. Ct. App. 1981)

FACTS

Mildred and Harold Rosengrant were an elderly couple living on a farm in Tecumseh, Oklahoma. They had no children of their own, only six nephews and nieces. One nephew, Defendant Jay Rosengrant, lived close to the couple and helped them from time to time. After Mildred was diagnosed with cancer, she called Jay to meet her and Harold at the bank whereby Jay was introduced to the couple's banker for the purpose of signing a deed to "the place" to him. The deed was subsequently signed and handed to Jay. They instructed Jay to return the deed to the banker, who put it in an envelope labeled "J. W. Rosengrant or Harold H. Rosengrant" in a safe-deposit box. The couple told Jay that he could record the deed when they died. In July 1974, when Mildred death was immanent, Jay consulted an attorney concerning the legality of the transaction. The attorney said the delivery seemed valid enough but told Harold he could nonetheless draw up a Will. After Harold died of lung cancer in January 1976, Jay obtained the deed from the bank and recorded it. A petition to challenge the transfer was filed in February 1978 by another relative (plaintiff) to cancel and set aside the deed. Plaintiff argued that the deed was null and void because it was never legally delivered and, alternatively, that it was void for failure to comply with the Statute of Wills because it was a testamentary instrument, operative only upon recordation after the death of the grantors. The trial court agreed holding the deed null and void. Defendant Jay Rosengrant appealed.

I Is there a valid delivery of a deed from the grantor to the grantee when (1) the grantor delivers a deed but retains a right of reclamation and (2) asserts that the deed is only effective only after his (the grantor's) death?

R Where a grantor delivers a deed but retains the right of reclamation and maintains that the deed is effective only after his death, the delivery is not legally binding; rather it is an example of symbolic delivery.

A Where a grantor delivers a deed but retains the right of reclamation and maintains that the deed is effective only after his death, the delivery is symbolic and not legally binding. Harold and Mildred intended to create legal delivery of the deed by handing it to Jay. Post "transfer," Harold continued to live on the farm and pay property taxes. He continued to exercise control over the property until his death. Thus, the words written on the envelope create the inescapable conclusion that the deed was retrievable by Harold any time before his death; an understanding that the deed was to take effect only upon the death of the couple. Thus, where a grantor delivers a deed under which he reserves a right of retrieval and attaches to that delivery a condition that the deed is to become operative only after he grantor's death and further continues to use the property as if no transfer occurred, the grantor's actions are nothing more than an attempt to employ the deed as a will.

C Where a grantor delivers a deed but retains the right of reclamation and maintains that the deed is effective only after his death, the delivery is not legally binding. Affirmed.

TITLE ASSUARANCE: THE INDEXES

Luthi v. Evans

223 Kan. 622, 576 P.2d 1064 (1978)

FACTS

Grace V. Owens and other parties collectively owned interests in several oil and gas leases located in Coffey County, Kansas. On February 1, 1971, Owens signed all of her interests in the leases to Plaintiff-Appellee International Tours Inc. (Tours) executed via a written instrument designated "Assignment of Interest in Oil and Gas Leases." This assignment provided in part that Owens and the other assignors intended to convey "all interest whatsoever of working nature in all Oil and Gas leases in Coffey County, Kansas;" language commonly referred to as a "Mother Hubbard" clause. This instrument was filed and recorded in the

County office of the registrar of deeds on February 16, 1971 (the "Tours Assignment"). In addition to the leases explicitly summarized in the Tours assignment, Owens owned a working interest in an oil and gas lease known as the Kufahl lease located in Coffey County. The Kufahl lease was not explicitly described in the instrument, but nevertheless fit the description in the Tours Assignment. On January 30, 1975, Owens executed and delivered a second assignment (the "Burris Assignment") of her interest in the Kufahl lease to Defendant-Appellant J. R. Burris. Burris personally checked the records in the office of the Registrar of Deeds before the second assignment occurred. After the assignment, Burris acquired an abstract of title to the same property. The prior assignment to Tours was not revealed by either his personal inspection of the records or via the abstract he obtained. Tours argues that the Tours Assignment successfully conveyed Owen's interest the Kufahl lease to Tours and that its February 16, 1971 filing gave such constructive notice to all later purchasers, including Burris. Burris argues that the notice was ineffective as the language of the assignment provided a poor description of the interest conveyed. The District Court held for Burris. On appeal, the Court of Appeals held that general description in the 1971 assignment was sufficient, when recorded, to provide constructive notice to all subsequent purchasers, including Defendant Burris. Defendant Burris appealed to the Kansas Supreme Court.

I Is an assignment incorporating a "Mother Hubbard" clause which describes an assigned interest sufficient to provide constructive notice to subsequent purchasers?

R An instrument which contains a Mother Hubbard clause is valid, enforceable and effectively transfers the entire property interest between the parties but is not effective to give constructive notice to subsequent purchasers and mortgagees who do not have actual knowledge of it.

A An instrument which contains a Mother Hubbard clause is valid, enforceable and effectively transfers the entire property interest between the parties but is ineffective to give constructive notice to subsequent purchasers and mortgagees who do not have actual knowledge of it. We also make it clear that in a situation where an instrument of conveyance containing a sufficient description of the property conveyed is duly recorded but not properly indexed, the fact that it was not properly indexed by the register of deeds will not prevent constructive notice under Kansas law. In the instant case, we agree that the Tours Assignment represented a legally binding transfer of Owens' interest in the Kufahl lease to Tours, but only as between those two parties to that assignment. Similarly, a single instrument can convey separate tracks by specific disposition or by general description which can be made specific. This is seen when the language of the assignment expresses that clear intent. The Registrar of Deeds is required by statute to keep a general index of title including a description of each tract conveyed. Also, a numerical index of all deeds including a brief description of the properties involved is required by statute. The statutes are intended to alert a subsequent purchaser notice of instruments which affect the title to a specific tract of land. Thus, a collective reading of all the statutory provisions taken together indicate that the legislature most likely intended that recorded instruments describe the conveyed land sufficiently well enough such that the specific land could be identified later on. Thus, an instrument utilizing a Mother Hubbard clause is invalid as to succeeding buyers, unless they have actual knowledge of the transfer. It may be used for emergency purposes, provided that the grantee takes precautions to defend his title against later buyers; such as securing possession of the property or via the filing an affidavit with the county describing the property in greater detail. In this case, because Burris took possession with actual notice of the Tours Assignment, the Burris Assignment prevails.

C An instrument which contains a Mother Hubbard clause is valid, enforceable and effectively transfers the entire property interest between the parties but is not effective to give constructive notice to subsequent purchasers and mortgagees who do not have actual knowledge of it. Judgment of District Court affirmed.

Orr v. Byers

198 U.Cal. App. 3d 666, 244 Cal. Rptr. 13 (1988)

FACTS

In October 1978, Plaintiff James Orr obtained a judgment against Defendant William Elliott in excess of $50,000. Orr's attorney prepared a written judgment against the defendant, but identified the defendant as William Duane Elliot. That November, an abstract of the judgment was recorded in the Orange County Recorder's office as William Duane Elliot and William Duane Eliot; "Elliott" being misspelled as "Elliot" and "Eliot" with one "t" missing from each of the entries. This abstract was listed in the county Grantor-Grantee Index under those names only. Defendant later obtained title to a parcel property subject to plaintiff's judgment lien. When defendant sold that property to Rick Byers (defendant) in July 1979, a title search failed to reveal the abstract of judgment. Thus, the preliminary title report did not disclose plaintiff's judgment lien against Elliott and the sale of Elliott's land to defendant was not used to satisfy plaintiff's judgment lien. In February 1981, plaintiff filed suit against Byers, Elliott, and two additional entities, Pomona First Federal Savings & Loan Association and Imperial Bank, seeking a declaration of the rights and duties of all parties. Fundamentally, plaintiff wanted a judicial foreclosure of his judgment lien. Plaintiff argued that the defendants had constructive notice of the abstract of judgment through the doctrine of *idem sonans* ("having the same sound"). The trial judge denied plaintiff's request for declaratory relief and ruled that the doctrine was inapplicable. A formal judgment was filed in February, 1986, and plaintiff's appeal followed.

I Does an abstract of judgment containing a misspelled name convey constructive notice of its contents under the doctrine of *idem sonans*?

R Requiring the title searcher to examine the title records for alternate spellings of the grantor's name would create an undue burden on the transfer of property.

A Requiring the title searcher to examine the title records for alternate spellings of the grantor's name would create an undue burden on the transfer of property. Under the doctrine of *idem sonans*, even though a person's name has been inaccurately written, the identity of a person will be presumed from the similarity of sounds between the pronunciations of the correctly and incorrectly spelled names. Thus, absolute accuracy in spellings of names is not required in legal proceedings in light of the above. This doctrine, however, is inapplicable where the written name is material and the spoken name is of no consequence. In the instant case, the written name is clearly important. It would place a great burden on our judicial system and on the defendant if we were to require the defendant or any title searcher to search the records for different spellings of the given name. To be sure, placing this additional burden on the defendant or title searcher would be unjustifiable given the potentially daunting task of searching the records for all those who have identical names. Even today, not every name revealed by a search is relevant to the actual individual subject to a specific lien. Cross-comparing liens against various names with similar spellings and then checking to see if those liens affected the target property would create even more superfluous names. While modern automation and computer technology is presently used in title searches, these systems do not solve the problem; often they make the problem worst. Therefore, the burden should lie with the plaintiff-judgment creditor to take steps to ensure satisfaction of the judgment, including spelling the names of the debtor correctly on legal papers.

C Requiring the title searcher to examine the title records for alternate spellings of the grantor's name would create an undue burden on the transfer of property. Judgment affirmed.

TYPES OF RECORDING ACTS

Messersmith v. Smith

60 N.W. 2d 276 (1953)

FACTS

The Messersmiths, Caroline and her nephew, Frederick, each owned an undivided ½ interest in three sections of land in Golden Valley County, North Dakota. Prior to May 7, 1946, Caroline executed and delivered a quitclaim deed to the property to Plaintiff Frederick, which was not recorded until July 9, 1951. On April 23, 1951 Caroline executed a lease to Defendant Herbert J. Smith which was recorded on May 14, 1951. On May 7, 1951, Caroline executed a mineral deed containing a warranty of title for in undivided ½ interest in and to all oil, gas and minerals under the three sections of land. This deed was recorded on May 26, 1951. On May 9, 1951, defendant executed a mineral deed conveying interest conveyed by Caroline to E. B. Seale. This deed was also recorded on May 26, 1951. Caroline claims that she thought she was signing a transfer of royalties only. Defendant Smith paid a consideration of $1400 for the deed. After leaving, defendant discovered that the deed incorrectly stated the term "his heirs" instead of "her heirs." Defendant returned to Caroline's home the same day and explained the mistake to her. He then tore up the deed of prepared another one in the same form and with the error corrected. According to Smith's testimony, he took the deed to the same notary public to whom Caroline acknowledged the first deed and after the notary confirmed Caroline's acknowledgment by phone, placed his seal and signature on the deed. It was this second Caroline-Smith deed that Seale apparently relied upon when making his purchase of the ½ interest. Thereafter, Plaintiff Frederick Messersmith filed action to quiet title. Defendant Seale answered by claiming defendant's mineral deed void; that he was the purchaser without actual or constructive notice of Frederick's claim; that the deed was never acknowledged, not entitled to be recorded and was obtained by fraud, deceit and misrepresentation. Smith defaulted.

I Can an instrument (deed) which is improperly acknowledged still be recorded?

R An improperly acknowledged instrument is not entitled to be recorded.

A An improperly acknowledged instrument is not entitled to be recorded. The trial court found no evidence of fraud or misrepresentation with respect to the execution of both deeds, and we agree. This case presents the unusual situation whereby two deeds conveyed the same property from the same grantor, who had no title, to the same grantee. The Smith-Messersmith deed was invalid because Caroline had already conveyed her interest to her nephew, Plaintiff Frederick Messersmith. The Smith-Seale conveyance was also invalid. The only way Defendant Seale can claim title in the property is by arguing that plaintiff's deed was not recorded until 1951. However, defendant employs faulty reasoning because his deed was nonetheless wrongly executed. Under North Dakota law, a deed to real property cannot be recorded without proper acknowledgment by the parties. Caroline did not appear before the notary and acknowledge she executed the deed that was recorded. Her alleged acknowledgment over the telephone was invalid nonetheless. Because the deed was not entitled to be recorded, the record then did not constitute notice of its execution and because the record did not constitute notice, the purchaser, Seale, did not become a subsequent good faith purchaser for value within the meeting of statute. The right the defendant attempts to claim is dependent exclusively upon compliance with the recording statute. His claim of title is similarly dependant upon the deed that was actually recorded, not on the one that was destroyed.

C An improperly acknowledged instrument is not entitled to be recorded. Judgment reversed.

CHAIN OF TITLE PROBLEMS

Board of Education of Minneapolis v. Hughes

118 Minn. 404, 136 N.W. 1095 (1912)

FACTS

On May 16, 1906, Carey B. Hoerger owned a lot which was subject to unpaid delinquent taxes. Defendant L. A. Hughes offered Carey B. Hoerger $25 for the lot, which was accepted by her; and defendant sent a $25 check to Carey's husband, along with the deed to be executed and returned. The name of the grantee on the deed was left blank. The Hoergers executed and acknowledged this deed on May 17, 1906 and mailed it back to defendant. The grantee's name on the deed was still left blank. Hoerger did not cash the defendant's check. On April 27, 1909, real estate brokers Duryea and Wilson paid Mrs. Hoerger $25 for a quitclaim deed to the same lot; which was executed and delivered. On November 19, 1909, Duryea and Wilson executed and delivered a warranty deed to the lot to Plaintiff Board of Education of Minneapolis. The Board recorded this deed on January 27, 1910. Defendant Hughes finally filled in his own name on his deed before recording it on December 16, 1910. Duryea and Wilson recorded their deed from Hughes on December 21, 1910. Evidence was not presented as to why none of these parties, with the exception of the Board, failed to file their deeds promptly.

I Does a deed from a grantor outside the chain of title give constructive notice to subsequent purchasers?

R A deed which is outside the chain of title does not give constructive notice to subsequent purchasers and is regarded as unrecorded, even if it was recorded. (This essentially the rule of the "wild deed").

A A deed which is outside the chain of title gives no constructive notice to subsequent purchasers and is regarded as unrecorded, even if it was recorded. It is well settled that a deed that does not contain a name is a nullity and is wholly inoperative as a conveyance until the name of the grantee is filled in. Thus, the deed to Hughes was inoperative as a conveyance until his name was inserted as grantee. Defendant Hughes had implied authority to fill in the blank space for the name because a grantee is presumed to have the authority to do so when the grantor retains consideration for the deed and delivers the deed to the grantee, as we have seen Hughes do here. The delay in filling in the name has no bearing on the validity of the instrument. As to the Board's claim of ownership, the facts support defendant's claim to title. When the property was deeded to the Board on November 19, 1909, there was no record showing Duryea and Wilson had any title to convey and that deed was not recorded until December of the following year. Defendant Hughes, on the other hand, was a subsequent purchaser and is thus protected by the fact that his deed was recorded five days prior to the Hoergers-Duryea/Wilson deed. On the day Hughes recorded his deed, the chain of title did not list Duryea and Wilson as record owners. Thus, Defendant Hughes was the rightful owner of the lot.

C A deed which is outside the chain of title does not give constructive notice to subsequent purchasers and is regarded as unrecorded, even if it was recorded. Order reversed and the trial granted.

Guillette v. Daly Dry Wall, Inc.

367 Mass. 355, 325 N.E.2d 572 (1975)

FACTS

Wallace L. Gilmore sold lots in a subdivision to the plaintiffs (the "Guillettes"), defendant and two others in May 1968 by a deed referring to a plan dated in March 1968. Prior to this transaction, Co-Plaintiff (the "Walcotts") purchased a lot from Gilmore in August 1967 by a deed referring to a plan dated in July 1967. Both plans were similar and did not mention any restrictions. In June 1968, Co-Plaintiff (the "Paraskivas") purchased a lot in the subdivision by a deed referring to the 1968 plan. Restrictions were contained in these three deeds, along with five others to lots in the subdivision. Gilmore and his neighbors intended to keep the subdivision limited to single-family residential use.

In April 1972, Defendant Daly Dry Wall Inc. purchased a lot from Gilmore. This deed did not reference any of the restrictions but referred to the 1968 plan. Defendant did not know of any development pattern in the subdivision and made no inquiries as to any restrictions on the property. Defendant only learned of the restrictions in August 1972 after a title examination was made. Thereafter, defendant obtained a building permit for 36 apartment units. Plaintiffs Guillette, the Walcotts, and the Paraskivas sued to enjoin the defendant from erecting the building. The court entered a final decree prohibiting defendant from building any structures not in conformity with the restrictions contained in the Gilmore-Walcott deed. Defendant appealed.

I Is a purchaser property in a subdivision bound by restrictions contained in deeds to neighbors from a common grantor when the purchaser took title without knowledge of the restrictions under a deed to him which did not mention the restrictions?

R A purchaser of property in a subdivision from a common grantor has constructive notice of the restrictions on the rest of the subdivision, and thus acquires title subject to those restrictions.

A A purchaser of property in a subdivision from a common grantor has constructive notice of the restrictions on the rest of the subdivision and thus acquires title subject to those restrictions. The deed from Gilmore to the plaintiffs conveyed the described lot in addition to the interest in the land then owned by Gilmore. What remained (that remaining land still owned by Gilmore but not yet sold) was subject to the same restrictions as the rest of the property. Thus, as a purchaser of part of the land, defendant took title subject to those restrictions. Defendant argued that charging him with notice of any restriction would be to impose the almost impossible task of searching each and every deed which a grantor deeded out in the subdivision. While arduous, it's not impossible. Even so, the Daly deed referred to the same plan as was mentioned in the Guillette deed. Thus, defendant was on constructive notice as to the existence of the restrictions in the subdivision.

C A purchaser of property in a subdivision from a common grantor has constructive notice of the restrictions on the rest of the subdivision, and thus acquires title subject to those restrictions. Decree affirmed.

PERSONS PROTECTED BY THE RECORDING SYSTEM

Daniels v. Anderson

162 Ill.2d 47, 642 N.E.2d 128 (Ill. 1994)

FACTS

In 1977 Plaintiff William A. Daniels contracted to buy two lots from Defendant Stephen Jacula. The contract gave Daniels the right of first refusal if defendant ever decided to sell an adjacent parcel for the same price as any prospective buyer offered. Plaintiff received and recorded the deed, but the right of refusal was not mentioned nor was the contract of sale recorded. In 1985, Defendant Zografos contracted with Defendant Jacula to buy the adjoining parcel for $60,000, but Plaintiff Daniels was not notified of the offer. Zografos paid Jacula $10,000 and gave defendant a note for $50,000. Zografos paid a total of $30,000 in early 1986. In June 1986 plaintiff's wife told Zografos of the right of first refusal. In August 1986 Zografos paid the outstanding $20,000 to Jacula and Zografos received a recorded the deed to the parcel. Plaintiff sued both defendants for specific performance of his preemptive option. Zografos contended that he was a bona fide purchaser without notice of the option. The trial court disagreed and held that he was not because he, Zografos, had actual notice of the option at the time he took title. The court ordered the conveyance of the parcel from Zografos to plaintiff and ordered plaintiff to pay Zografos the $60,000 purchase price plus $11,000 in property taxes Zografos had already paid out. Defendant Zografos appealed and invoked the doctrine of equitable conversion arguing, in effect that he was a bona fide purchaser because he took equitable title in September 1985 before he was the legal owner of the contiguous parcel in August 1986. The Appellate Court reversed, holding that defendant waived his right to advance this theory because he did not assert it prior to appeal. Zografos appealed to the Supreme Court of Illinois.

I At what point during the executory stage of a real estate installment contract does a buyer become a bona fide purchaser when he receives notice of an outstanding interest after paying less than the full purchase price?

R A purchaser becomes a bona fide purchaser only after the full purchase price has been paid.

A During the executory stage of a real estate installment contract, a buyer who receives notice of an outstanding interest subsequent to paying some, but not all of the full purchase price is not considered a bona fide purchaser. A bona fide purchaser takes title to real property without notice of the interests of others. A majority of jurisdictions have applied a pro tanto rule which protects the buyer to the extent of the payments made prior to notice, but no further. This is true even though some appellate courts have held that partial payment of the consideration is insufficient to render the buyer a bona fide purchaser. Thus, we hold that the trial court's determination of the ownership issue was fair and not an abuse of discretion.

C A purchaser becomes a bona fide purchaser only after the full purchase price has been paid. Affirmed.

Lewis v. Superior Court

30 Cal. App. 4th 1850 (Cal. Ct. App. 1994)

FACTS

In February 1991, Robert and Josephine Lewis (plaintiffs) contracted to buy a home for $2.3 million from one Shipley. A few days before the Lewises took title, Fontana Films (defendant) recorded a lis pendens (notice of lawsuit affecting title to the property) on the property on February 24. The Lewises paid $350,000 in cash on February 25th and closed October 28, 1991 after the plaintiffs gave Shipley a note for the balance due. Up until this point, the plaintiffs did not have actual nor constructive notice of the lis pendens. The lis pendens was indexed on February 29, 1991. Thereafter, the plaintiffs fully paid off the note and renovated the property at a cost over one million dollars. By September 1993, the Lewises were informed of the lis pendens for the first time when they were served with defendant's lawsuit. Plaintiffs sued to remove the lis pendens and clear their title. Defendant Fontana Films argued that plaintiffs were not bona fide purchasers because the property was not fully paid for until after the indexing of the lis pendens; even though they took title prior to the indexing. The trial court disagreed and denied the plaintiff's motion for summary judgment. An appeal followed.

I If a buyer has not paid for the property in full, can he still be considered a bona fide purchaser?

R A seller need not be fully paid before the buyer can be considered a bona fide purchaser.

A A seller need not be fully paid before the buyer can be considered a bona fide purchaser. Defendant erroneously relies on our out-of-date holding in *Davis v. Ward* (a buyer becomes a bona fide purchaser only upon full payment). But the *Davis* rule is out-of-step with current real property law. The rule advanced in *Davis* was partially based on the idea that a buyer who loses his land was "not injured" if he has not "paid in full" for the property. This claim is economically irreconcilable with a contemporary purchaser's expectations as any buyer who makes a down payment without notice of any lien or encumbrance, and clearly obligates himself to pay the outstanding amount due, should be confident that, if the payments timely made, his right to the property will be protected. The *Davis* court acknowledged that a buyer could be a bona fide purchaser if the bank was given a note in exchange for a mortgage because the seller would have been paid in full. In contrast, a buyer who gave the seller a note could only be considered a bona fide purchaser when he made his final payment to the seller. This distinction is illogical because it punishes a buyer for a cash transaction with the seller. Order denying the plaintiff's motion for summary judgment is vacated and a new order granting the motion is issued.

C A seller need not be fully paid before the buyer can be considered a bona fide purchaser.

Alexander v. Andrews

135 W. Va. 403, 645 S.E.2d 487 (W. Va. 1951)

FACTS

Mary and Thomas Alexander each owned a ½ share in their home as of June 1945 as tenants in common. When Mary died in April 1946, she devised her ½ interest to Plaintiff Charles Alexander, her son. On May 8, 1946, Thomas delivered a deed for his ½ interest to Defendant Sarah Andrews (the "Thomas-Sarah deed"), his daughter, for "love and affection." On May 14, 1946 Thomas delivered a second deed for his interest to his son Charles (the "Thomas-Charles deed"), even though Thomas had a ready transferred his interest to his daughter one week earlier. Charles recorded the deed on May 14, 1946. Consideration for the Thomas-Charles deed (the second deed) was (1) Charles's $1000 payment made prior to May 14; (2) his promise to care for Thomas until his death; and (3) to pay for Charles's burial costs. Plaintiff Charles promptly recorded his deed but Defendant Sarah did not record her deed until July 8, 1946. Thomas died in October, 1948. Plaintiff Charles Alexander claimed to have no notice of the Thomas-Sarah deed, and he wished to quiet title to his property using West Virginia's Recording Act. Defendant Sarah Andrews argued that Charles's conveyance was void because he did not render full consideration before she (Sarah) recorded her deed.

I (1) Must a succeeding grantee have completed the transaction for the sale of land by tendering full consideration prior to the recordation of the deed by original grantee? (2) Is the subsequent grantee permitted to recoup the consideration he already paid out if the prior grantee acquires title to the property?

R In a race-notice jurisdiction, any later grantee must complete his transaction by paying valuable, reasonable and adequate consideration in order to benefit from the recording act before the original grantee records and a later grantee can obtain reimbursement of that consideration paid out if the prior grantee obtains legal title.

A (1) In a race-notice jurisdiction, any later grantee must complete his transaction by paying valuable, reasonable and adequate consideration in order to benefit from the recording act before the original grantee records. The West Virginia Recording Act protects grantees who take title without notice of a prior deed; record the deed before the original grantee records; and render full and adequate consideration necessary to support the transfer. In the instant case, Plaintiff Charles Alexander had no notice of the Thomas-Sarah deed when he obtained and recorded his deed from Thomas. Moreover, he recorded his deed before Sarah recorded hers. However, Charles did not complete his transaction. The evidence shows that Charles only paid $1000 for the ½ interest received; an interest that had a reasonable value of $3850. Accordingly, the $1000 payment was not enough to constitute full consideration. The balance of the consideration owed was to come from plaintiff's actions in caring for Thomas until his death. Turning to the Thomas-Sarah deed, we note that after Sarah's deed was recorded, it became effective for all purposes. Thus Charles, the grantee in Thomas-Charles deed, not having completed his purchase, could not obtain rights based upon the payments already made. (2) A later grantee can obtain reimbursement of that consideration paid out if the prior grantee obtains legal title. In the instant case, plaintiff never received legal title to the instant property as the deal had not been completed at the time Sarah recorded her deed on July 8. However, plaintiff had already paid $1000 and cared for Thomas in expectation of acquiring the land. As a result, Charles is entitled to the refund of the full $1000 by defendant for and for any sums spent in caring for his father until July 8, 1946.

C In a race-notice jurisdiction, any later grantee must complete his transaction by paying valuable, reasonable and adequate consideration in order to benefit from the recording act before the original grantee records and a later grantee can obtain reimbursement of that consideration paid out if the prior grantee obtains legal title. Remanded.

INQUIRY NOTICE

Harper v. Paradise

233 Ga. 194, 210 S.E.2d 710 (Ga.1974)

FACTS

On February 1, 1922, Susan Harper conveyed by warranty deed a 106.65 acre farm to Maude Harper, her daughter-in-law for life, remainder in fee simple to Maude's named children, including Plaintiff-Appellant Clyde. The deed was lost or misplaced and not recorded until July 1957, when plaintiff found it and recorded it. Susan died sometime during the period 1925-1927 and was survived by her heirs. John Harper was the only heir who didn't execute a deed to Maude which was recorded in 1928. This deed specifically memorialized that the earlier deed was lost. Five years later, Maude executed a deed conveying the property to Ella Thornton as security for a loan. Ella foreclosed after Maude defaulted. In 1936, Ella received a sheriff's deed which was recorded that same year. Thus, a continuous chain of tile existed between Ella and the Paradises (defendant-appellees) who were the grantees to the 1955 deed; a deed recorded that same year. Defendants claim direct title from the deed from Susan's heirs to Maude and claim title by adverse possession, which they argue began in 1940. Clyde argues that defendant's title is invalid because the 1928 deed put all parties on notice of the earlier deed. Maude died in 1972. Defendants received a directed verdict and Clyde appealed.

I Are later grantees presumed to have inquiry notice of the subject matter of prior recorded deeds?

R In a race-notice recording jurisdiction, ensuing grantees are considered to have inquiry notice of the subject matter of prior recorded deeds in the chain of title.

A In a race-notice recording jurisdiction, later grantees are considered to have inquiry notice of the subject matter of prior recorded deeds in the chain of title. In the instant case, the 1928 deed explicitly referenced the 1922 deed to Maude. As a result, Maude is considered to have taken the 1928 deed with notice of the 1922 deed. The narration in the 1928 deed put any subsequent buyer on notice of the earlier 1922 deed. Therefore, the 1928 deed is not entitled to priority, despite the fact that it was recorded before the 1922 deed. Moreover, the defendants cannot rely on the 1922 deed, because any interest potentially obtained under this deed would be Maude's life estate, which terminated upon her death in 1972. We thus hold that it was up to the defendants to learn, through a careful examination, the contents of the 1922 deed because the 1928 deed provided constructive notice of its existence. Defendants did not do so. Defendants made no effort to ascertain the interest conveyed in the 1922 deed when they bought the property in 1955. What's more, defendants cannot claim title by adverse possession beginning in 1942 because the statute would not have begun to run until 1972, the year of Maude's death.

C In a race-notice recording jurisdiction, ensuing grantees are considered to have inquiry notice of the subject matter of prior recorded deeds in the chain of title. Reversed and remanded; judgment to be entered in favor of plaintiff.

Waldorff Insur. & Bonding, Inc. v. Eglin National Bank

453 So. 2d 1383 (Fl. Dist. Ct. App. 1984)

FACTS

Choctaw Partnership (Choctaw) developed certain properties in Okaloosa County, Florida by constructing condominiums. On June 8, 1972, Choctaw executed a promissory note and mortgage on the properties for $850,000. The note and mortgage was then assigned to Plaintiff-Appellee Eglin National Bank (Eglin) in January 1975. At the time, a $41,562.61 principal balance remained due on the note and the mortgage. In April 1973, Defendant Waldorf Insurance and Bonding Inc. entered into a purchase agreement with Choctaw to buy condo Unit 111 and occupied the unit in April or May 1973, and continually occupied and maintained the unit for 1½ years thereafter. In October 1973, Choctaw executed a note and mortgage for the principal sum of $600,000 in favor of the Bank. Unit 111 was included. Choctaw was a client of Waldorff and in March 1975, Choctaw agreed to consider the purchase price of Unit 111 as paid in full in exchange for defendant's satisfaction of Choctaw's past-due debt for insurance premiums owed by Choctaw to the Defendant Waldorff. Choctaw executed a quitclaim deed in favor of the defendant and defendant wrote off the debt on its taxes. Eglin foreclosed against Choctaw in 1976. While the final judgment was entered in September of that same year, jurisdiction was retained to settle the ownership issue regarding Unit 111. Seven years later, a hearing on the ownership issue was commenced and the trial court ruled that plaintiff held superior title to Unit 111; that defendant's occupancy of Unit 111 was "equivocal" because Choctaw allowed several other condo units to be used by persons who had no interest in the units, and that defendant did not pay adequate consideration for Unit 111, such that its quitclaim deed was void. Defendant filed this appeal.

I Are those who claim adverse possession of some property on constructive notice of an ownership interest by others who are in actual possession?

R Actual possession gives all parties constructive notice of any right which the party in possession is able to establish.

A Actual possession puts all adverse claimants on constructive notice of an ownership interest in a piece of property. In the instant case, at the time the Choctaw Partnership executed both of the mortgages in the Bank's favor, the defendant openly and exclusively occupied Unit 111. Therefore, the Bank is deemed to have had constructive notice of defendant's adverse title, such that the Bank cannot claim any benefits stemming from the recording act. It is of no significance to this case that the other condo units were occupied by persons without legal or equitable title because each unit was intended to be conveyed as a separate, individual and independent parcel. The plaintiff argues that it would have been near impossible for it to determine if the defendant actually owned Unit 111. We disagree. Although it would have been difficult for the Bank to find out who truly owned Unit 111, the *Phelan v. Brady* (actual possession of real estate is sufficient to a person proposing to take a mortgage on the property and to all the world, of the existence of the right which the person in possession is able to establish) holding is controlling here. Moreover, we rule that the trial court incorrectly held that the conveyance from Choctaw to Waldorff Insurance lacked consideration and was thus void due. This error is evidenced by the fact that Choctaw was relieved from payment of the debt and that this relief constituted valuable consideration in and of itself. Thus, we are left with only the Bank's 1972 mortgage lien and deem it superior to any of the defendant's interests. We note that the satisfaction of this lien can come from the 1976 foreclosure sale of the other condo units. We therefore hold that defendant's title is superior to the other mortgages.

C Actual possession gives all parties constructive notice of any right which the party in possession is able to establish. Reversed and remanded.

TITLE INSURANCE

Walker Rogge, Inc. v. Chelsea Title & Guaranty Co.

116 N.J. 517, 562 A.2d 208 (1989)

FACTS

Plaintiff Walker Rogge Inc. bought a track of land from Alexander Kosa, through its president, John Rogge, who had acquired the land from one Aiello. Before the purchase, Kosa showed John Rogge a 1975 survey by Price Walker which assessed the track at 18.33 acres. The sale contract, however, referred to the survey but suggested the track was "19 acres more or less." The track was priced at $16,000 per acre, adjusted for the deviations in acreage, plus the cost of an existing house, for a total price of $363,000. As time was of the essence, the contract was signed on December 12, 1979 and closed on December 31. Rogge hired Defendant Chelsea Title & Guaranty Company (Chelsea) to do the title work on his behalf. Defendant was familiar with the property as it had issued two prior title policies on the property. Chelsea's files contained a copy of the Aiello-Kosa deed which declared that the property contained only 12.486 acres. Both the Kosa-Rogge deed and Chelsea's title insurance policy referenced the Price Walker survey, but did not indicate the lot's acreage. The terms of the policy stated that Chelsea would insure plaintiff against any loss or damage which "could result if the title were vested differently from what was stated in the policy; if any defect on the title existed, and if the title was unmarketable." However the policy did not insure against loss or damages which "could be disclosed by an accurate survey and inspection of the premises." By 1985, plaintiff had hired a surveyor to examine the adjoining parcels. This survey confirmed that plaintiff's track was actually 12.43 acres. Thereafter, plaintiff filed this action, arguing that the acreage slippage was an insurable "loss" and that Chelsea was negligent in failing to disclose the true acreage of the lot. The trial court found that the policy covered the acreage shortage; that there was a defect in title; that the title was unmarketable and that the survey exception was meaningless. Damages were awarded. The appellate division affirmed, but remanded for damages.

I Can a title company be held liable for not disclosing the results of its title examination to the insured?

R A title company that fails to conduct a reasonable title examination, or having done so, fails to disclose the results to the insured may be liable under the terms of the insurance policy but not in tort for negligence.

A Title companies guarantee title, not acreage. Thus, if a title company fails to conduct a reasonable title search and examination, or having conducted an examination fails to disclose the results to the insured, then it can be found liable under the terms of the insurance policy. That being said, we find the survey exception here is neither vague nor unenforceable. Generally, title policies are read in favor of the insured and liberally construed against the insurer. Even so, any buyer of real estate runs risk of not receiving all the land he or she pays for without a proper surveyor. Thus, title insurance is no substitute for a comprehensive survey and the insured should provide the title company with a suitable survey to avoid future problems. Had this been done in the instant case, such a survey would have exposed the acreage short fall. Turning our attention to the issue of liability, we note that in our State, a title company is only liable under the terms of the policy itself and not for negligence in searching any records. The logic behind this rule is that the title company's obligations and legal responsibilities depend on the contractual relationship between the insurer and insured. The record indicates that Chelsea was only asked to prepare a title insurance policy and that the title search performed by Chelsea was incidental to that request. The title search was purely an in-house process done for defendant's own benefit. While there is a split of authority as to whether a title company should be liable for negligence under its policy if it does not disclose specific information of value to the insured, we believe that the relationship between the two is fundamentally contractual in nature leading to the creation of the insurance policy itself. To that end, an insured expects that if it pays its premiums promptly and those payments are not in arrears, it will be fully insured under the terms of policy. Therefore, a title company that fails to make or disclose the results of a reasonable <u>title examination</u> may be found liable under the policy. Thus, Defendant Chelsea Title could be held liable for the acreage shortfall only if it assumed duties <u>in addition</u> to those duties outlined in the insurance policy <u>and</u> damages resulted. The trial court did not determine whether defendant assumed an independent duty to assure the quality of the acreage of the track as a result of its earlier policies on the property; whether it breached that duty or whether the breach caused Rogge to sustain any damage. Therefore we remand to the trial court on those issues.

C A title company that fails to conduct a reasonable title examination, or having done so, fails to disclose the results to the insured may be liable under the terms of the insurance policy but not in tort for negligence. Judgment of the appellate division affirmed in part, reversed in part and remanded.

Lick Mill Creek Apts. v. Chicago Title Insur. Co.

231 Cal. App. 3d 1654, 283 Cal. Rptr. 231 (1991)

FACTS

In 1979, Kimball Small Investments (KSI) purchased property upon which various companies operated warehouses and chemical plants in the past and where underground tanks, pumps and pipelines were used in handling hazardous substances eventually contaminating the soil, subsoil and groundwater. The California Department of Health Services ordered KSI to clean up the pollution, but KSI did not comply. Seven years after KSI's initial purchase of the property in question, Plaintiff Lake Mill Creek Apartments (LMCA) bought a parcel of the property (Lot 1) from KSI and bought title insurance from Defendant Chicago Title Insurance Co. (Chicago Title) to insure it. As part of the insurance process, defendant had a survey and inspection of the property prepared prior to issuing the policy. LMCA thereafter bought Lots 2 and 3 from KSI and hired Chicago Title for those policies as well. All the lots were surveyed and inspected revealing the presence of the pollution. At the time of the issuance of the policies, records revealing the existence of toxic substances on the property existed at the Department of Health Services and other state and local agencies. LMCA paid for all the decontamination costs relating to the Lots and then sued Chicago Title for reimbursement of those costs. Plaintiff argued that the presence of the contaminated materials impaired the property's marketability of title and that its presence was an encumbrance on the title such that the policy should pay for the losses sustained by LMCA. The defendant denied coverage and the trial court sustained the defendant's demurrer. This appeal followed.

I Should a title insurance policy pay out when the physical conditions of the property adversely affect the marketability of the land and increase the likelihood of the owner paying out additional costs?

R Title insurance policies protect an owner from defects relating to the title to the land but do not provide insurance for the physical condition of the land itself.

A Title insurance policies protect an owner from defects relating to title to land but do not provide insurance for the physical condition of the land itself. In the instant case, LMCA's position on the marketability of their title is unsupported because it is based upon a view that marketable title somehow encompasses the market value of the property and that this broad view is in some way legally significant. We find no support for this position. The concept of the marketability of title to land is different from the notion of the market value of the land. Thus, an owner's failure to make viable fiscal use of his land stemming from a prior violation does not cause the title to be defective nor render the land unmarketable under a standard insurance policy. In this case, plaintiff only protested those conditions affecting the marketability of the land, but not those affecting the title. LMCA therefore cannot claim coverage under its policy for harms arising from the physical state of the property. The fact that the property is polluted and had to be cleaned up at considerable expense to LMCA does not mean that an encumbrance on the title must therefore exist. An encumbrance is a lien, easement, restrictive covenant or an interest held by a third person(s) and we refuse to enlarge this definition to include the existence of harmful material. The fact that the government might impose a lien on the property in the future does not mean there is or will be a defect, lien or encumbrance on the title.

C Title insurance policies protect an owner from defects relating to the title to the land but do not provide insurance for the physical condition of the land itself. Judgment affirmed.

X. LAND USE

A. Zoning

A state, through its enabling act, has zoning powers. All zoning ordinances must be authorized by the state's legislature and will be held valid unless they are arbitrary and unreasonable, having no substantial relation to the public health, safety, morals or general welfare. Additionally, zoning ordinances must be enacted with notice or there will be a violation of due process and thus the ordinance will be held unconstitutional.

B. Support

All landowners must maintain support for the benefit of adjacent lands. If an excavator is negligent in causing improved land to cave in, he is liable for any damages. Strict liability attaches to an excavator if his actions would have caused the cave in of the property in its natural state.

C. Waste

Waste is a commission or omission by one in possession of land. There are three types of waste on land:

1. Voluntary Waste

Voluntary waste is an affirmative, willful action by one in possession of land via the stripping its value.

2. Permissive Waste

Permissive waste is committed by the omitted actions of a possessor of the land.

3. Ameliorative Waste

Ameliorative waste is when one in possession of land actually enhances its value.

D. Water Rights

1. Allocation of Water in Watercourses

There are two major theories for the allocation of water in watercourses. Eastern states follow the Riparian Water Right Doctrine, whereas western states follow the Prior Appropriation Doctrine.

a. Riparian Water Rights
Under this doctrine, water in watercourses belongs to those who own the land bordering the watercourse and the water can only be used in connection with that parcel. There are two theories for riparian rights, the Reasonable Use Theory and the Natural Flow Theory.

- **Reasonable Use Theory**
  Under the Reasonable Use Theory, a riparian owner is subject to liability for making unreasonable use of the water in a watercourse that causes harm to another riparian owner's reasonable use of the water. There are several factors that are used to determine the reasonableness of the use of the water. They are: purpose of the use, where the water is being taken from and the extent of the use.

- **Natural Flow Theory**
  Under this theory, a riparian owner is entitled to the use of adjacent watercourses in their natural condition.

b. Prior Appropriation Doctrine
Under this minority theory, priority is determined by the first person to arrive and use the watercourse.

2. Underground Water
There are three different rules for determining underground water rights: reasonable use, absolute ownership and appropriation rights.

a. **Reasonable Use Doctrine**
The Reasonable Use Doctrine is the majority view. Under this doctrine, a proprietor of land may withdraw underground water for a beneficial purpose and is not subject to liability for interference with the use of another's water use unless: (1) the withdrawal of water causes harm to a neighbor; (2) the withdrawal of water is not for a reasonable use; or (3) the withdrawal has a direct effect on the watercourse.

b. **Absolute Ownership Doctrine**
An owner of land can take as much water from under his property as he wishes for any purpose.

c. **Appropriate Rights Doctrine**
Under this doctrine, the first to use the water has the priority right.

3. **Surface Water**
An owner of land may use surface water that is within his boundary line for any purpose. There are three theories for the use of surface water:

a. **Common Enemy Theory**
Under this theory, an owner of property may take protective measures to get rid of surface water.

b. **Natural Flow Theory**
Under this theory, owners of property cannot alter natural drainage patterns.

c. **Reasonable Use Theory**
Under this theory, a balancing test is used to determine the reasonableness of the use of the surface water. Specifically, the utility of the use is balanced against the harm caused.

E. **Eminent Domain**
Eminent domain allows the federal and state governments to take title to private property against the owner's will. However, the taking must be for public use and reasonable compensation must be paid to the owner for the property.

Morgan v. High Penn Oil Co.

(1953) 238 N.C. 185, 77 S.E.2d 682

FACTS

Prior to August 1945, Plaintiff Morgan acquired a track of land which contained a dwelling house. Immediately after purchasing the land, plaintiff built a restaurant and trailer park on the land and rented both to third persons. Plaintiff also rented space in his home for additional income. Beginning in October 1950, High Penn Oil Co. (defendant) operated an oil refinery approximately 1000 feet from plaintiff's property. In addition, within a one mile radius of the refinery was located a church, at least 29 homes, a plant nursery and various small businesses. Two or three days a week, the refinery emitted large amounts of nauseating gasses and odors into the surrounding air. People "of ordinary sensitiveness" within a radius of 1 ¼ miles of the refinery were rendered uncomfortable and sick by these gasses. Plaintiff's use and enjoyment of his land and those to whom he rented were thus substantially impaired. Plaintiff and others situated nearby insisted that High Penn stop the emissions immediately, but defendant did not. Defendant argued that its use of the oil refinery is part of its business; that its business was a lawful enterprise and thus halting the refinery's operation was not actionable at law because it was not an abatable private nuisance. Defendant also argued that the refinery can only be considered a nuisance if it was constructed or operated in a negligent manner. A jury disagreed, found the refinery to be nuisance and awarded $2500 and damages. The trial judge entered a judgment to that effect and enjoined the defendant from continuing to operate the refinery. Defendant appealed.

I If an otherwise lawful enterprise is not constructed or operated in a negligent manner, may it still be considered a nuisance *per accidens* (an otherwise lawful act or structure which can become a nuisance by virtue of its location) or a nuisance in fact?

R A private nuisance exists when one improperly uses his own property in a way that injures the land or some incorporeal right of another; that is, where there is a substantial interference with the use and enjoyment of another's land which is either intentional or unintentional and is the result of negligence, recklessness or an abnormally dangerous activity.

A The existence of negligence is not a prerequisite to maintain or create a nuisance *per accidens* also known as a "nuisance in fact." A private nuisance exists when one improperly uses his own property in a way that injures the land or some incorporeal right of another; that is, where there is a substantial interference with the use and enjoyment of another's land which is either intentional or unintentional and is the result of negligence, recklessness or an abnormally dangerous activity. In the instant case, the refinery is a lawful enterprise and thus cannot be regarded as a nuisance *per se*. However, it can be considered a nuisance *per accidens*; even when negligence has not been proven or alleged. The law of private nuisance rests on the concept embodied in the legal maxim *Sic utere tuo ut alienum non laedas* (every person should use his or her own property so as not to injure another). When a person acts with the specific purpose of causing the nuisance or knows that the nuisance is substantially certain to result from his or her conduct, that intrusion into a person's private use and enjoyment of the land is considered intentional. Therefore, when a party intentionally produces or sustains a private nuisance, he is liable for the ensuing harm irrespective of the level of skill employed to circumvent such harm. In the instant case, it is apparent that the defendant both deliberately and unreasonably caused injurious gases and odors to escape from its plant significantly impairing plaintiff's use and enjoyment of his land. In addition, the proof offered by the plaintiffs demonstrates that defendant aims to maintain the operation of the refinery in the same manner thus continuing to impose lasting injury on the plaintiff and his use and enjoyment of his property. Plaintiff is therefore entitled to mandatory or prohibitory injunctive relief as may be required to prevent High Penn Oil from continuing the nuisance.

C A private nuisance occurs where there is a substantial interference with the use and enjoyment of another's land by one who is using his own land improperly. Judgment affirmed.

Estancias Dallas Corp. v. Schultz

(1973) 500 S.W.2d 217

FACTS

In early 1969, an eight building apartment complex containing 155 rentable units was completed next to the home of Plaintiffs Thad Schultz and his wife in the city to Houston. Thereafter, Defendant Estancias Dallas Corp. began operating a large, single air conditioning unit which served the entire complex. The unit was located 5 ½ feet from the plaintiff's property line and about 70 ft. from their bedroom. According to the testimony proffered, the unit sounded like a jet airplane or helicopter when operational. The noise was so loud that it prevented the plaintiffs from carrying on normal conversations within their home with all the doors and windows closed and also interferes with their sleep at night. Plaintiffs testified that as a result of this noise, the value of their property dropped $15,000 from $25,000 to $10,000. The original owner of the apartment complex claimed that this air conditioning system cost about $80,000 to construct; that separate AC units for each of the eight buildings would have totaled $120,000; that the cost of conversion to this latter system would have been between $150,000 and $200,000 and that these apartments could not be rented without air conditioning. We note that at the time, there was no shortage of apartments in the city of Houston. The jury found that the noise generated by the equipment constituted a permanent nuisance and the court issued a permanent injunction against the defendant and awarded $10,000 in interim damages to the plaintiff. Defendants appealed, arguing the court had erred in its holding because it failed to balance the equities.

I Can a court appropriately grant an injunction for a permanent nuisance to the complaining party if the harm sustained by that party is less than the harm the party causing the nuisance would suffer from the issuance of the injunction?

R An injunction remedy for nuisance will be denied only if the necessity of others compels an injured party to seek damages in an action at law and not because the defendant has the right to hurt others.

A A court must balance the equities when considering whether or not to grant an injunction. Applying this approach, the court will consider both the potential harm to the defendant and to the public if an injunction is granted as balanced against the harm to the plaintiff if the injunction is denied. We follow this well-established rule as created by the Texas Supreme Court in *Story v. Central Hide and Rendering Company* (even though a jury finds facts constituting a nuisance, there should be balancing of equities to determine whether an injunction should be granted). Thus, if an injunction is not granted, it will not be because the party causing the nuisance has the right to injure his neighbor. Instead, the nuisance will be allowed to continue and the injunction seeking relief denied only if the court finds that the necessity of others which compelled the injured party to seek damages in an action at law is absent. However, the *Story* Court placed great emphasis on the public interest; holding, in effect, that an injunction could be granted even if it would cause only minor injury to the public and to the nuisance-causing party when balanced against to the harm suffered by the moving party. In the instant case, there is no proof that the apartment availability in the city of Houston is scarce. As such, there is no evidence to suggest that the public would be harmed needlessly or be left homeless should this one apartment complex go without its loud air conditioning system. Moreover, there is no evidence to suggest that plaintiffs' to request for relief via an action for damages rather than a request for an injunction is justified.

C An injunction remedy for nuisance will be denied only if the necessity of others compels an injured party to seek damages in an action at law and not because the defendant has the right to hurt others. Judgment affirmed.

Boomer v. Atlantic Cement Co.

(1970) 26 N.Y.2d 219, 257 N.E.2d 870, 309 N.Y.S.2d 312

FACTS

Atlantic Cement Company (ACC) operated a large cement plant near Albany, New York. Neighboring land owners (plaintiffs) including Plaintiff Boomer alleged damage to their property interests as a result of the high levels of dirt, smoke and vibration that the plant produced. The trial court held that a nuisance was present and awarded temporary damages to the neighbors in exact sums until the trial commenced. The trial court denied the plaintiffs' request for injunction because it reasoned that the total damage sustained by plaintiffs was small compared to damage that an injunction would exact upon the defendant. Plaintiffs were also awarded a monetary sum of $185,000 for permanent damages.

I Should a court resolve the litigation between the parties in terms of an equitable remedy or should the court, seeking the promotion of the public welfare, channel private litigation into broad public objectives? That is, should a court grant an injunctive remedy for a nuisance when the injunction would have greater economic ramifications for the party causing the nuisance than for the party complaining of the nuisance?

R A court may grant an injunction conditioned on the payment of permanent damages to the injured party in order to compensate the party for the harm caused by the nuisance to the complainant's respective property rights.

A A court may grant an injunction conditioned on the payment of permanent damages to the injured party in order to compensate the party for the harm caused by the nuisance to the complainant's respective property rights. The trial court denied an injunction because of a large inequality in economic consequences between imposing the injunction and denying the injunction. The trial court's awarding of damages, however, disregards the historical doctrine that an injunction should be granted where a nuisance has been established and where the plaintiff has suffered considerable injury. But if we adhered to the letter of the law, this rule would require the closing of the plant. Alternatively, we could grant the injunction but postpone its result until after a period of time. This option would allow time for as yet to be developed advances in technology to stop the nuisance without closing the plant. But there is no guarantee that such advances will ever be developed and until that time the created harm persists. Thus, the best alternative is to issue the injunction and require ACC to pay the plaintiffs permanent monetary damages to be set by the court. It is within our power to do so. Permanent damages are permitted when the amount the moving party could recover is less than the cost of completely removing the nuisance. In reality, defendant would be purchasing "a servitude" on the plaintiffs' land whereby future recovery by the plaintiffs or their grantees would be foreclosed. Judgment reversed.

C A court may grant an injunction conditioned on the payment of permanent damages to the injured party in order to compensate the party for the harm caused by the nuisance to the complainant's respective property rights.

Spur Industries, Inc. v. Del E. Webb Development Co.

(1972) 108 Ariz. 178, 494 P.2d 700

FACTS

The area located along Grand Avenue; roughly 15 mi. west of the urban center of Phoenix was first put into agricultural use in 1911 and was used primarily for farm-related activities until the late 1950s. Four years later, the retirement community of Youngtown was established in the region for senior citizens. By 1956, feedlots were developed about 2 ½ miles south of Grand Avenue and by mid 1959, between 7,500 and 8,500 head of cattle were being fed there. In May 1959, Plaintiff Del E. Webb Development Co. (Webb) commenced development on a residential community known as Sun City using 20,000 acres of farmland it previously purchased; land that was less expensive than the land closer to Phoenix. One year later, Defendant Spur Industries Inc. (Spur) bought the feedlots and began an operational and geographic expansion program. In early 1960, Webb offered these newly built homes for sale, situated just 2 ½ miles north of the Spur lots. Four months later, roughly 500 houses were either completed or in the process of being built. Ironically, at this juncture, Plaintiff Webb did not consider the smells emanating from defendant's feedlots to be problematic and continued its expansion south of Grand Avenue. By 1962, the feedlots grew to 114 acres from 35. By December 1967, defendant's lots were within 500 ft. of Webb's property. Only Plaintiff Webb filed an action to enjoin defendant's operation of the feedlots, arguing it was public nuisance; the citizens of Sun City and Youngstown did not. At the time of the complaint, 20,000 to 30,000 head of cattle were being fed producing over 1,000,000 lbs. of manure per day. Although the defendant employed suitable housekeeping practices with regard to the lots, the odor and flies nonetheless created an annoying, if not unhealthy situation. The citizens of Sun City eventually complained about the situation and Webb faced sales resistance with regard to selling new homes in the area.

I (1) Can a lawful activity become a nuisance because others have moved into the area after the commencement of the activity and thus be subject to the nuisance? (2) Assuming such an activity can be enjoined, should the injunction-requesting party be required to provide compensation for the cost of ending the activity?

R A lawful activity can become a nuisance and thus be enjoined if others thereafter entered the zone of activity; however, if the party requesting the injunction created the need for the injunction, that party can be required to provide compensation for relocating or halting the nuisance-causing activity.

A (1) Yes. A lawful activity can become a nuisance and thus be enjoined if others thereafter entered the zone of activity. A public nuisance is one that affects the rights enjoyed by the general public. In the instant case, we are persuaded that the feedlots constituted both a public and private nuisance to the extent that the Sun

City residents were involved. Arizona State law §36-601 codifies public nuisances as including "any conditional place in populous areas which constitutes a breeding place for flies, which are capable of carrying and transmitting disease-causing organisms to any person or persons." Accordingly, Sun City fulfills the "populous area" element of the law. Additionally, we note that the plaintiff lost sales, a real and apparent injury, such that it had standing to bring this action. (2) Yes. The complaining party can be required to provide recompense to the nuisance-causing party for the cost of relocating or ceasing the activity. It is important to note that a court of equity is charged with the protection of all parties' interests, not just the public's interest. As such, the interests of a lawful business operation whose activities thereafter become a nuisance because of the encroachment of others must also be protected. In these so called "coming to the nuisance" cases, the law has held the complaining party may not obtain relief if it came to an area with knowledge that the area was used or to be used for industrial or agricultural development. But the law is flexible to advance what is fair and practical under a given set of facts. In the instant case, the evidence shows that Spur Industries and its predecessors in title were unaware at the time their feedlot operation commenced that an entire city would be built around them forcing them to move and defendant must move its operations because it is in the public's interest to do so. Similarly, plaintiff is entitled to relief because of the damage caused by the defendant's feedlot activities upon the Sun City residents. However, it would be inequitable to allow Webb, a real estate developer, who has already received the benefit of low rural land prices to build a city and then use the existence of that city as a tool to neutralize a nuisance without paying the offender. We stress, however, that this type of relief is narrowly drawn and applied to specific causes of action where a developer has brought in those very residents which cause the once lawful activity to become a nuisance. Thus, having brought people to the nuisance to the foreseeable detriment of Spur, Webb must indemnify Spur for a reasonable amount of the cost of moving or shutting down.

C A lawful activity can become a nuisance and thus be enjoined if others thereafter entered the zone of activity; however, if the party requesting the injunction created the need for the injunction, that party can be required to provide compensation for relocating or halting the nuisance-causing activity. Judgment affirmed in part, reversed in part, and remanded.

XI. MORTGAGES

A mortgage is an interest in land created in an instrument providing security for the performance of a duty or the payment of a debt. The mortgage must be signed and in writing to satisfy the statute of frauds. The parties to a mortgage are the mortgagor (who is the debtor) and the mortgagee (who is the lender, e.g., a bank). If the mortgagor does not pay the mortgage debt on time, the mortgagee may claim title to the property or sell the property and keep the proceeds to satisfy the debt. Any obligation capable of being reduced to its monetary equivalent may be secured by a mortgage.

A. TYPES OF MORTGAGES

1. Purchase Money Mortgage

A purchase money mortgage is a mortgage that a buyer gives the seller when the property is conveyed to secure the unpaid balance of the purchase price.

2. Equitable Mortgage

An equitable mortgage is a mortgage where property is posted as security for a loan and the deed is transferred to a creditor to be reconvened if the debt is not paid.

3. Recourse Mortgage

This is a mortgage where the mortgagor is personally liable to the mortgagee for any deficiency in the event of a foreclosure.

4. Non-recourse Mortgage

This is a mortgage where the mortgagor is not personally liable to the mortgagee for any deficiency in the event of a foreclosure.

B. Taking Property Subject to the Mortgage or Assuming the Mortgage

If a seller conveys property to the buyer without satisfying the mortgage, the grantee will take the property either subject to the mortgage or by assuming the mortgage.

1. Subject to the Mortgage

When a buyer takes property subject to the mortgage, the buyer is not personally liable for the mortgage debt. If the mortgage is not paid, the mortgagee may foreclose on the property.

2. Assuming the Mortgage

When a buyer takes property and assumes the mortgage of the seller, he is personally liable for the debt. The mortgagee may therefore hold either the buyer or the seller liable for the full debt. If, however, the mortgagee holds the seller liable, the buyer will be liable to the seller since he assumed the debt.

C. Termination of the Mortgage

A mortgage may be terminated by the following:

1. Payment

If the debt is paid in full, the mortgage is satisfied and the mortgage note is terminated.

2. Merger

If the mortgagor and the mortgagee merge their interests, the mortgage is terminated.

3. Foreclosure

Foreclosure is an equitable remedy when the mortgagor defaults on the mortgage. This is one option a mortgagee may use to recover any and all money lent to the mortgagor to purchase the property. In a foreclosure, the property is sold and the proceeds are used to satisfy the debt. If the proceeds are insufficient to satisfy the debt, the mortgagee may bring a personal action against the mortgagor for the deficiency.

If the mortgagor defaults on a mortgage payment, a majority of jurisdictions allow for a redemption of the property. However, a minority of jurisdictions do not. The right of redemption allows the mortgagor the opportunity to pay off the mortgage and keep the property. There are two types of redemption:

a. **Redemption in Equity**
Redemption in equity allows the mortgagor to redeem the mortgaged property if he pays off the entire mortgage before the foreclosure sale.

b. **Statutory Redemption**
Statutory redemption allows the mortgagor to redeem the mortgaged property if the mortgage is paid in full within the statutory period of time, which could range from six months to one year.

If there are multiple mortgages on a piece of property, the first mortgage is called the senior mortgage and all subsequent mortgages are called junior mortgages. In the event of a foreclosure initiated by the senior mortgagor, only junior mortgages that are named in the foreclosure may collect to satisfy their debt. If a junior mortgage is not named in the foreclosure action, it must wait until other debts are paid before its debt can be satisfied.

THE MORTGAGE

Murphy v. Financial Development Corp.

126 N.H. 536, 495 A.2d 1245 (1985)

FACTS

Plaintiffs (the "Murphys") bought a house in 1966 and secured a mortgage to pay for it. By March 1980, the Murphys refinanced the mortgage, executing a new promissory note and a power of sale to mortgagee Defendant Financial Development Corp. (FDC). In February 1981, plaintiff lost his job and the Murphys were seven months in arrears on their mortgage payments. FDC unsuccessfully discussed options to assist plaintiffs in making their payments but on October 6, 1981, FDC gave notice of its intent to foreclose. Plaintiff thereafter paid the late payments but not the costs and legal fees of the foreclosure proceedings. Nevertheless, Defendant set the foreclosure sale for November 10, 1981 at the home site and met all the legal prerequisites for notice. At the plaintiffs' request, and for an additional fee of $100, defendant deferred the sale until December 15, 1981 and notice of the sale was posted at the property, at the local City Hall, at the post office and for three weeks in the local newspaper. At 10 a.m. on December 15, the appointed time of the sale, the only people in attendance were the plaintiffs, an FDC representative, and Morgan Hollis, an attorney filling it in for the defendant's attorney. The FDC representative made the only bid at the sale, $27,000; the amount owed on the mortgage including costs and fees. The bid was accepted and the sale was ended. Later that same day, one of Morgan Hollis's clients, a corporation, offered to buy the property from FDC for $27,000. Defendant countered with an offer of $40,000, but two days later the property was sold for $38,000 to the corporation. On February 5, 1982, the Murphys sued FDC and FDC moved to dismiss. The Master found that FDC failed to exercise good faith and due diligence in obtaining a fair price for the property. Finding the market value to be $54,000, the Master calculated damages at $27,000 and assessed legal fees to FDC on account of bad faith. FDC appealed.

I Must a mortgagee exercise due diligence and act with good faith when setting a price at a foreclosure sale of mortgaged property?

R A mortgagee is under an affirmative duty to protect the interests of the mortgagor and exercise due diligence and good faith in obtaining a fair price for a mortgagor's property in a foreclosure sale.

A The mortgagor's duty is that of a fiduciary; where the modern trend has been to liberally define the term "fiduciary" to prevent unjust enrichment. A mortgagee, therefore, must exert a reasonable effort when executing a power of sale to protect the interests of the mortgagee while exercising good faith and due diligence in obtaining a fair price for a mortgagor's property. What constitutes a fair price, then, is the key question upon which this case turns and will depend on the circumstances of each case. Inadequacy of a fair price alone is not sufficient to demonstrate bad faith unless the price is so low as to "shock the conscience of the court." However, where is "an intentional disregard of duty or a purpose to injure" bad faith exists. In the instant case, FTC complied with the legal requirements of notice and carried out the sale in conformity with similar stipulations. FDC also delayed the sale once, did nothing to hinder other buyers, and made its bid unaware of any other present or immediate buyer. These facts reveal that FTC did not act with bad faith. With only advertisements at the property itself and at selected public places and without any real bidders at the sale, FTC was able to purchase the house and make an immediate profit. This is true despite the fact that FTC did not have a specific buyer for the property at the time of the sale. Even so, the fact that FDC sold the house for so much more than it had paid reinforces the fact that FTC had to know it was able make such a profit. This awareness is the most convincing evidence that FDC did not act with bad faith but rather failed to exercise due diligence in obtaining a fair price for the property. Thus, where a mortgagee fails to exercise due diligence, as opposed to bad faith, damages are assessed as the difference between a fair price for the property and the price obtained at the foreclosure sale. We note that this calculation is different where bad faith is evident. In cases of bad faith, damages are calculated as the difference between the *fair market value* of the property and the actual price obtained at the sale.

C A mortgagee is under an affirmative duty to protect the interests of the mortgagor and exercise due diligence and good faith in obtaining a fair price for a mortgagor's property in a foreclosure sale. Judgment reversed in part, affirmed in part, and remanded.

Bean v. Walker

95 A.D.2d 70, 464 N.Y.S.2d 895 (1983)

FACTS

In January 1973, the Beans (plaintiffs) agreed to sell a single family home in Syracuse, New York to the Walkers (defendants) for $15,000. The sale contract provided that the $15,000 was to be paid over a 15-year period at 5% interest, in monthly installments of $118.62 each. The plaintiff-sellers retained legal title to the property and agreed to convey it to the defendants when full payment of the purchase price was completed according to the terms of the contract, thus allowing the defendant-buyers possession of the property only. The contract contained an acceleration clause whereby if the defendants defaulted in making payment and failed cure that default within 30 days, the plaintiffs could demand the full balance due or terminate the contract and repossess the property. If the Beans chose to terminate the contract in the event of a default, the Beans could retain all the money paid by the Walkers up to that point as "liquidated damages" under a forfeiture clause. This money would be applied to the rent. In January 1973, the defendants went it to possession of the house and thereafter made substantial improvements on the property. They made all of the required payments under the contract until August 1981, when Carl Walker became injured and could no longer work eventually triggering a default. Defendants had paid the plaintiffs $12,099.24, with $7,114.75 of it being applied to the $15,000 principal up until the time of the default. Thus, at the time of the default, the Walkers had paid almost one-half of the principal to the defendants. After the required 30 day period allotted to the Walkers to cure, this action was filed by the Beans seeking an action granting them ownership of the land. The court granted summary judgment to the plaintiffs.

I Does a buyer who defaults on a payment in an installment land sale contract automatically forfeit prior payments to the seller and lose possession of the property?

R If forfeiture would result in the inequitable disposition of property and an exorbitant money loss by the buyer, equity can and should intervene to stop forfeiture of the buyer's payments because a buyer in an installment land sale contract obtains equitable title which must be eliminated before the seller can retake possession.

A If forfeiture would result in the inequitable disposition of property and an exorbitant money loss by the buyer, equity can and should intervene to stop forfeiture of the buyer's payments because a buyer in an installment land sale contract obtains equitable title which must be extinguished before the seller can retake possession. In *Skendzel v. Marshall* (vendee in land sale contract requires equitable title and contract is consummated) the Indiana Supreme Court held that the parties in an installment land sale contract are not unlike that of a mortgagor and mortgagee. This status strongly suggests that the concept that equity should apply here as well. Thus, the critical question for us to decide is whether the buyer in an installment land sale contract has acquired a property interest that must be eliminated before the seller may retake possession. In the instant case, the defendants acquired equitable title and the plaintiffs held the legal title in trust for them. Therefore, the plaintiffs in this case had to foreclose the equitable title or bring an action at law for the purchase price in order to retake possession. The Beans pursued neither of these alternatives. Therefore, should we allow the lower court's judgment to stand, the plaintiffs would be allowed to retake the property after improvements by the defendants, in addition to the $11,000 in principal and interest payments already paid out by the Walkers. This result would be clearly inequitable. Thus, equity should be applied when forfeiture would lead to an unfair disposition of property and an exorbitant loss of money would occur.

C If forfeiture would result in the inequitable disposition of property and an exorbitant money loss, equity can and should intervene. Judgment reversed, motion denied, and matter remitted.

TABLE OF AUTHORITIES

INDEX

A

B

C

D

E

F

G

H

I

J

K

L

M

N

O

P

Q

R

S

T

U

V

W

Z